PUERTO PLATA
SOSÚA CABARETE

Benoit Prieur
Pascale Couture

Travel better, enjoy more
ULYSSES
Travel Guides

Author Benoit Prieur Pascale Couture	*Page Layout* *Typesetting* Tara Salman Alain Legault	*Photography* *Cover Page* Grant V. Faint Image Bank
Editor Daniel Desjardins	*Visuals* Anne Joyce	*Inside Pages* Tibor Bognar Alain Legault
Project Director André Duchesne	*Cartographers* Patrick Thivierge Yanik Landreville	M. Daniels A. Cozzi Morandi Sappa
Translation Janet Logan Stéphanie Lemire	*Illustrations* Myriam Gagné Lorette Pierson	*Artistic Director* Patrick Farei (Atoll)
English Editing Tara Salman	Marie-Annick Viatour	*Computer Graphics* Stéphanie Routhier

Distributors

AUSTRALIA: Little Hills Press, 11/37-43 Alexander St., Crows Nest NSW 2065, ☎ (612) 437-6995, Fax: (612) 438-5762

BELGIUM AND LUXEMBOURG: Vander, Vrijwilligerlaan 321, B-1150 Brussels, ☎ (02) 762 98 04, Fax: (02) 762 06 62

CANADA: Ulysses Books & Maps, 4176 Saint-Denis, Montréal, Québec, H2W 2M5, ☎ (514) 843-9882, ext.2232, 800-748-9171, Fax: 514-843-9448, info@ulysses.ca, www.ulysses.ca

GERMANY and AUSTRIA: Brettschneider, Fernreisebedarf, Feldfirchner Strasse 2, D-85551 Heimstetten, München, ☎ 89-99 02 03 30, Fax: 89-99 02 03 31, cf@brettschneider.de

GREAT BRITAIN and IRELAND: World Leisure Marketing, Unit 11, Newmarket Court, Newmartket Drive, Derby DE24 8NW, ☎ 1 332 57 37 37, Fax: 1 332 57 33 99, office@wlmsales.co.uk

ITALY: Centro Cartografico del Riccio, Via di Soffiano 164/A, 50143 Firenze, ☎ (055) 71 33 33, Fax: (055) 71 63 50

NETHERLANDS: Nilsson & Lamm, Pampuslaan 212-214, 1380 AD Weesp (NL), ☎ 0294-494949, Fax: 0294-494455, E-mail: nilam@euronet.nl

PORTUGAL: Dinapress, Lg. Dr. Antonio de Sousa de Macedo, 2, Lisboa 1200, ☎ (1) 395 52 70, Fax: (1) 395 03 90

SCANDINAVIA: Scanvik, Esplanaden 8B, 1263 Copenhagen K, DK, ☎ (45) 33.12.77.66, Fax: (45) 33.91.28.82

SPAIN: Altaïr, Balmes 69, E-08007 Barcelona, ☎ 454 29 66, Fax: 451 25 59, altair@globalcom.es

SWITZERLAND: OLF, P.O. Box 1061, CH-1701 Fribourg, ☎ (026) 467.51.11, Fax: (026) 467.54.66

U.S.A.: The Globe Pequot Press, 246 Goose Lane, Guilford, CT 06437-0480, ☎ 1-800-243-0495, Fax: 800-820-2329, sales@globe-pequot.com

OTHER COUNTRIES, contact Ulysses Books & Maps (Montréal, Canada)

No part of this publication may be reproduced in any form or by any means, including photocopying, without the written permission of the publisher.

Canadian Cataloguing in Publication Data (see page 8)
© January 2000, Ulysses Travel Publications.
All rights reserved
Printed in Canada
ISBN 2-89464-308-X

*"...En verdad.
Con tres milliones
suma de la vida
una entre tanto
cuatro cordilleras cardinales
y une inmensa bahía y otra inmensa bahía,
tres penínsulas con islas adyacentes
y un asombro de ríos verticales
y tierra bajo los árboles y tierra
bajo los ríos y en la falda del monte
y al pie de la colina y detría del horizonte
y tierra desde el canto de los gallos
y tierra bajo al galope de los caballos
y tierra sobre el día, bajo el mapa, alrededor
y debajo de todas las huellas y en medio del amor.
Entonces
es lo que he declarado.
Hay un país en el mundo
Sencillamente agreste y depoblado..."*

– Pedro Mir
Hay un país en el Mundo, 1913

"...In truth.
With three million
lives in total
to which can be added
four cardinal mountain ranges
and one large bay and another large bay,
three peninsulas with orbiting islands
and a surprising number of vertical rivers
and land under the trees and land
under the rivers and on the mountain slopes
and at the foothills and beyond the horizon
and land from the calling of the roosters
and land under the horses' gallop
and land over the day, and under the map, all around
and under every footstep and even in the heart of love.
So
didn't I tell you.
There is
one country in this world
Quite simply rural and unpopulated...

– Pedro Mir
There is one country in this World, 1913
(Our translation)

Table of Contents

Portrait 11
    Geography 12
    Fauna 14
    History 17
    Politics 32
    Economy 34
    Population 36
    Culture 37
    Traditions 37

Practical Information 43
    Entrance Formalities . 43
    Embassies 44
    Consulates 44
    Tourist Offices 46
    Entering the Country 47
    Insurance 48
    Health 49
    Climate 53
    Packing 54
    Safety 54
    Security 54
    Mail &
      Telecommunications 63
    Tour Guides 65
    Holidays 65
    Taxes 66
    Tips 66
    Electricity 66
    Women Travelling
      Alone 66
    Smokers 66
    Gay Life 66
    Prostitution 67
    Time Change 67
    Weights and
      Measures 67
    The Semana Santa .. 68

Outdoors 69
    National Parks 69
    Outdoor Activities .. 72

Exploring 83
    Puerto Plata 84
    Costambar 89
    Playa Cofresí 89
    Playa Dorada 90
    Puerto Chiquito 90
    Sosúa 91
    Punta Goleta 92
    Cabarete 92
    Gaspar Hernández .. 93
    Playa Magante 93
    Río San Juan 94
    Playa Grande 95
    Cabrera 95
    The Palm Tree Route 96
    Nagua 96
    Excursion to Santo
      Domingo 96
    Excursion to
      Jarabacoa 109

Accommodations 111
    Types of
      Accommodation .. 111
    Apart-hotels 112
    Cabañas 112
    Bed and Breakfasts 112
    Youth Hostels 112
    Puerto Plata 112
    Playa Cofresí 114
    Playa Dorada 115
    Sosúa 118
    Cabarete 124
    Río San Juan 128
    Playa Grande 130
    Cabrera 130
    Nagua 130

Restaurants 131
    Dominican Cuisine . 131
    Drinks 131
    Puerto Plata 132

Restaurants (ctd...)
- Playa Dorada 135
- Sosúa 135
- Cabarete 137
- Río San Juan 139
- Cabrera 139
- Jarabacoa 142

Entertainment 143
- Puerto Plata 143
- Playa Dorada 143
- Sosúa 144
- Cabarete 144

Shopping 145
- Opening Hours . . . 145
- Alcohol 145
- Mercados 145
- Puerto Plata 145
- Playa Dorada 146
- Sosúa 146
- Cabarete 146

Glossary 148

Index 155

List of Maps

Beaches around Puerto Plata	73
Cabarete	125
East of Puerto Plata	10
Geographical Situation	9
Playa Dorada	116
Puerto Plata and Sosúa (Colour Map)	inset
Puerto Plata	85
Puerto Plata (Downtown)	87
Río San Juan	129
Santo Domingo (Downtown)	101
Santo Domingo	97
Sosúa	119
Table of Distances	57

Map Symbols

✈	Airport	⊘	Beach
🚌	Bus Terminal	🏌	Golf
H	Hospital	🏰	Fortaleza
⇌	Bridge	⋰	Ruins

Symbols

🚢	Ulysses' Favourite
☎	Telephone Number
⇄	Fax Number
≡	Air Conditioning
⊗	Fan
⊛	Whirlpool
≈	Pool
ℜ	Restaurant
ℝ	Refrigerator
♠	Casino
K	Kitchenette
tv	Colour Television
pb	Private Bathroom
½b	Half Board
bkfst	Breakfast Included

ATTRACTION CLASSIFICATION

★	Interesting
★★	Worth a visit
★★★	Not to be missed

RESTAURANT CLASSIFICATION

The prices in the guide are for a meal for one person, not including drinks and tip.

$	$10US and less
$$	$10US to $20US
$$$	$20US to $30US
$$$$	$30US and more

All prices in this guide are in US dollars.

Write to Us

The information contained in this guide was correct at press time. However, mistakes can slip in, omissions are always possible, places can disappear, etc. The authors and publisher hereby disclaim any liability for loss or damage resulting from omissions or errors.

We value your comments, corrections and suggestions, as they allow us to keep each guide up to date. The best contributions will be rewarded with a free book from Ulysses Travel Publications. All you have to do is write us at the following address and indicate which title you would be interested in receiving (see the list at the end of guide).

Ulysses Travel Publications
4176 Rue Saint-Denis
Montréal, Québec
Canada H2W 2M5
www.ulysses.ca
E-mail: info@ulysses.ca

Cataloguing

Canadian Cataloguing in Publication Data

Couture, Pascale, 1966-

    Puerto Plata, Sosúa

    2nd ed.
    (Ulysses Due South)
    Translation of: Puerto Plata, Sosúa, Cabarete
    Previously published as: Puerto Plata, Sosúa, Cabarete. 1994.
    Includes index.

    ISBN 2-89464-308-X

1. Puerto Plata (Dominican Republic) - Guidebooks. 2. Sosúa (Dominican Republic) - Guidebooks. 3. Dominican Republic - Guidebooks. I. Prieur, Benoit, 1965- . II. Title. III. Title: Puerto Plata, Sosúa, Cabarete. IV. Series.

F1939.P9P7413 1999   917.293'580454   C99-941811-4

"We acknowledge the financial support of the Government of Canada through the Book Publishing Industry Development Program (BPIDP) for our publishing activities".

We would also like to thank SODEC (Québec) for their financial support.

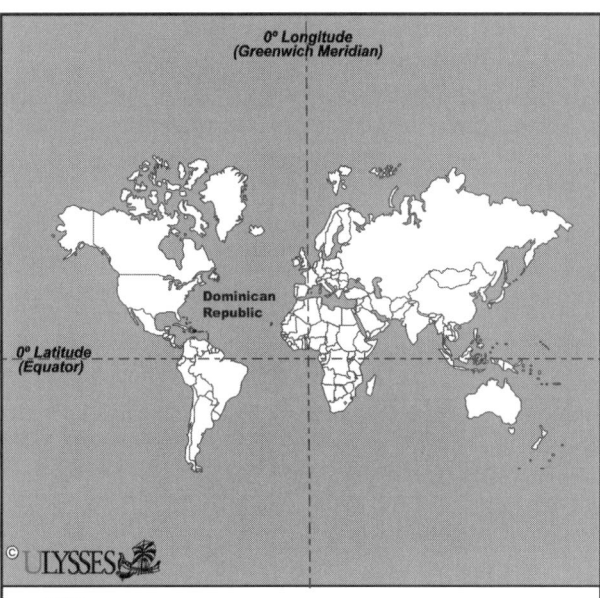

Where are *Puerto Plata and Sosúa* ?

Dominican Republic

Capital:	Santo Domingo
Language:	Spanish
Population:	8,000,000 inhab.
Currency:	Dominican peso
Area:	48,442 km²

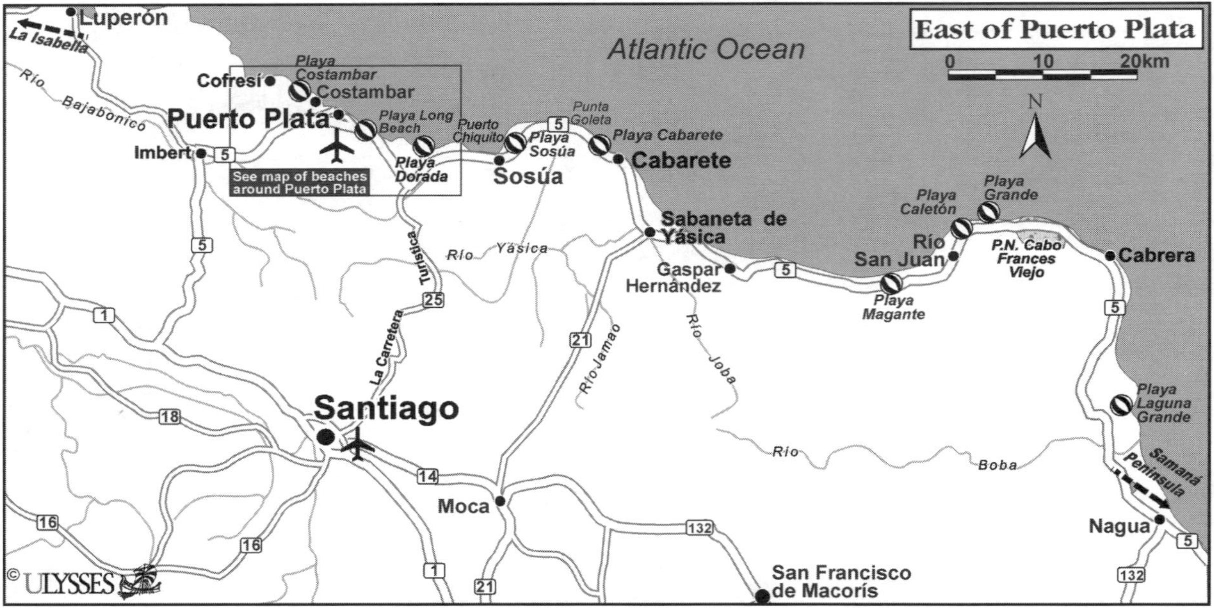
East of Puerto Plata
Atlantic Ocean
0
10
20km
N
Luperón
La Isabella
Río Bajabonico
Cofresí
Playa Costambar
Costambar
Puerto Plata
Playa Long Beach
Imbert
Playa Dorada
See map of beaches around Puerto Plata
Puerto Chiquito
Playa Sosúa
Sosúa
Punta Goleta
Playa Cabarete
Cabarete
Sabaneta de Yásica
Río Yásica
Turística
La Carretera
Gaspar Hernández
Playa Caletón
Playa Grande
Río San Juan
P.N. Cabo Frances Viejo
Cabrera
Playa Magante
Río Jamao
Río Joba
Playa Laguna Grande
Río Boba
Samaná Peninsula
Nagua
Santiago
Moca
San Francisco de Macorís
© ULYSSES

Portrait

The Dominican Republic shares with Haiti the island of Hispaniola, the second largest island in the Caribbean after Cuba.

Once the adopted land of the Tainos (Arawaks) and the Caribs, this island was "discovered" by Christopher Columbus and became home to the first European colony in the New World in 1492.

Known above all for the splendour of its white-sand beaches, the Dominican Republic is a country of tremendous diversity.

This guide only covers one region of the country – the north or Atlantic coast from Puerto Plata until, but not including, the Samaná Peninsula – covering some 150km of coastline.

Over the past 20 years, tourist development has been most intense on the north coast of the country. Many towns and villages have been converted into large resort towns. The north coast's beautiful beaches stretch past Puerto Plata, Sosúa and Cabarete all the way to Río San Juan and Playa Grande in the east.

Despite the north coast's popularity, its inhabitants go about their daily lives unhindered, practising the same economic activities that were the reason for settlement: fishing and agriculture.

Sparsely populated, the north coast still has wild expanses waiting to be discovered by the most adventurous.

Geography

With an area of 48,442km², the Dominican Republic occupies the eastern two thirds of the island of Hispaniola. When crossing the country, it is hard not to be seduced by the astonishing diversity of the countryside.

Mountains

Five mountainous massifs rise from the Dominican territory. The most impressive is the Cordillera Centrale at the heart of which stands Pico Duarte, which with an altitude of 3,175m is the highest summit in the Caribbean. Southwest of and extending from this range are two small mountain chains, called Neiba and Baoruco. To the north, the whole Atlantic coast is isolated from the rest of the country by the Cordillera Septentrionale, which runs from Monte Cristi to San Francisco de Macoris. Finally, spanning the Samaná Peninsula on the eastern part of the island, is the Cordillera de Samaná.

The Plains

In between these mountain ranges stretch vast plains ideal for agriculture and grazing. In fact, 40% of Dominican land serves as grazing ground for animals, while one third is dedicated to agriculture. Fields stretch as far as the eye can see, especially sugar-cane fields, which have shaped the Dominican economy and countryside for centuries. The largest of these plains is the Cibao valley, in the centre of the country. This fertile land, where corn, rice, beans and tobacco are grown, is the country's most important agricultural region.

Tropical Rainforest

The heavy precipitation and constant humidity and temperature (never under 20°C) at the foot of the Cordillera Centrale have engendered the growth of a tropical rain forest. Three levels of vegetation can be distinguished in this verdant world. The first level, called the underbrush, consists of woody plants (young unmatured trees and shrubs that can survive in the shade) and herbaceous plants. All of these plants thrive on the little light that manages to penetrate the canopy above them.

The second level consists of epiphytes (plants that do not touch the earth, but rather grow on other plants), such as mosses, lichens, creepers and bromeliads. These plants have adapted to dark and dank surroundings while making optimum use of the space available. Finally, the last level, the canopy, consists of the tallest trees in the forest, whose leaves absorb almost all of the solar energy. This forest is also populated by an incredible variety of animals, mostly birds and insects.

The Beaches

Most of the Dominican Republic's coastline is lined with beaches, in many cases of pristine sand. The prettiest beaches are located along the northern coast and are washed by the Atlantic Ocean, as well as in the Punta Cana region in the eastern extremity of the island.

A very particular vegetation grows along these beaches, made up essentially of creepers, sea-grape trees and coconut palms.

Mangrove Swamp

This strange forest grows in mud and salt water and consists essentially of a few varieties of mangrove, recognizable by their large aerated roots which plunge into the submerged earth. Farther inland, the river mangrove grows in less salty waters. Shrubs and plants also grow in these swamps. Amidst this impenetrable tangle of roots and vegetation live various species of birds, crustaceans and above all insects. The Gri-Gri Lagoon, in Río San Juan, is an excellent spot to view the astonishing ecosystem of the mangrove.

Mangrove

The Ocean Floor

The shallow, perpetually warm (about 20°C) waters just off the island provide a perfect environment for the growth of coral. Formed by a colony of minuscule organisms called coelenterate polyps growing on a polypary (calcareous skeleton), coral takes many different forms. The abundant plankton around these formations attracts a wide variety of marine wildlife. Fish of all sizes also gravitate around the coral. These include tuna, kingfish and on rare occasions sharks, plus more colourful fish like parrot-fish, boxfish, mullet and angel-fish. The coral is also home to numerous other animals, like sponges and sea urchins.

Fauna

Very few mammals, apart from rodents (rats and mice) and cattle, inhabit Hispaniola. The island separated very early from the American continent, and therefore has few of the indigenous species that evolved later on the mainland. In fact, most of the mammals here were introduced during the colonial era. Wild pigs were among the species imported during the colonization of the island, and can still be seen in certain parts of the country.

The **mongoose** was introduced onto the island by colonists in an effort to eliminate the snakes and rats that lived in the fields and attacked workers.

Mongoose

However, this little animal, which resembles a weasel, doesn't only hunt snakes (in fact, none of the island's snakes are really dangerous); it also goes after reptiles and ground-nesting birds, actually threatening the survival of some species. Mongooses can be spotted near fields, if you keep your eyes peeled.

Among the few species that inhabited the island before the arrival of colonists, the **agouti** is a small rodent from the shrew family, which is about the size of a hare. Their numbers are few, and they are spotted only rarely.

Reptiles are more common. You are sure to see some little lizards sunning themselves here and there. Another, much larger reptile, the **iguana**, can be observed in the desert-like expanses of the southwest. This animal, which feeds on plants and insects, can grow to up to one metre long. Don't be afraid, though; the iguana is harmless. **Turtles** inhabit various areas, especially the islands of Siete Hermanos, north of Monte Cristi. Finally, **American crocodiles**, found only in Lago Enriquillo, are the largest animals on the island. A few marine ammals populate the coastal waters, including the **manatee**, a bulky, gentle animal that resembles a large seal. Unfortunately, their numbers have diminished greatly in recent years, and they are spotted rarely.

Turtle

Humpback Whale

Another marine mammal, the **humpback whale**, which can grow to up to 16m, can be spotted near the coast of Bahía de Samaná. Arriving from the North Atlantic where they find an abundance of food during the summer, these whales head south to the warm waters of the Caribbean to reproduce (the gestation period lasts 12 months). Between January and March, whale-watching expeditions from Samaná allow visitors to become better acquainted with this fascinating mammal.

Winged wildlife abounds all over the island, making a bird-watcher out of just about anyone who looks around. To help you identify these animals, we have included a description of the most common species below. With a bit of patience and a good pair of binoculars, you are sure to spot a few.

The **brown pelican** has greyish brown plumage and is identifiable by its long neck, enormous bill and long grey beak. It is usually seen alone or in small groups, flying in single file. These birds, which can grow to up to 140cm, are commonly found near beaches.

The wingspan of the jet-black magnificent **frigate bird** can reach up to 2.5m. The colour of the throat is the distinguishing mark between the sexes; the male's is red, the female's white. These birds can often be seen gliding effortlessly over the waves in search of food.

Frigate

Herons are often found wading at the edge of ponds and mangrove swamps. Among the different types found in the Dominican Republic is the **great heron**, which can grow to up to 132cm tall. It is identifiable by the large black feather extending from its white head and down its neck. Its body is covered with grey and white plumage.

The **cattle egret** is another bird in the same family commonly seen on the island, usually in the fields among cattle. This bird is about 60cm tall, with white plumage and an orange tuft of feathers on its head. The cattle egret arrived in the Caribbean during the 1950s; before that it was found only in Africa. It has adapted well and is found in large numbers throughout the Caribbean.

Cattle Egret

Finally, you might hear the distinctive call of the **small green heron**, which stands about 45cm tall and has greenish-grey feathers on its back and wings.

The **pink flamingo**, another wader, is found along the shores of Lago Enriquillo. It feeds by turning its head upside down and dragging its beak through the mud while its tongue creates suction to trap small crustaceans and other organisms.

Coticas

Small green and red parrots called **coticas** can be seen in the gardens of several hotels. These domesticated birds are very popular with Dominicans, as they make friendly companions and can even learn to say a few words. The cotica, also known in Creole as the *verde cotorra*, is unfortunately being hunted into extinction.

The minuscule **hummingbird**, with its dark blue and green iridescent plumage, rarely grows more than 12cm long, and some types weigh no more than 2 grams. It feeds on insects and nectar, and can be seen humming about near flowering bushes and trees.

Hummingbird

The male **carib grackle** is completely black, while the female is paler. It is identifiable by its distinct yellow eyes. Its elongated claws allow it to run through fields in search of insects.

There are several types of **turtledoves** on the island, all about the size of a pigeon. The most widespread is the zenaida dove, with a brown back and a pinkish-beige breast, neck and head. It also has a blue spot on either side of its head. The common turtledove has greyish-brown plumage, with a black and white speckled neck.

The **bananaquit**, also known as a yellow-breasted sunbird, is a small bird, about 10cm tall, found throughout the Caribbean. It is easily identifiable by its dark grey or black upper-parts and its yellow throat and breast. It feeds on nectar and juice from various fruits including bananas and papayas. This greedy little bird often sits down on a patio table for a bit of sugar.

History

Well before the arrival of Christopher Columbus and the first Spanish conquistadors, large native populations inhabited the fertile island of Hispaniola. Like all native Americans, their ancestors were nomads from northern Asia who crossed the Bering Strait near the end of the ice age, and eventually inhabited almost all the American continent through successive waves of migration.

Between 5500 and 3500 BC, the Ciboneys came from South America and settled on the island of Trinidad. From there they slowly migrated to the other islands in the West Indies, arriving in Hispaniola around 2500 BC.

The First Inhabitants of the West Indies

When the first European explorers arrived, the majority of the West Indies was occupied by two native peoples, the Tainos and the Caribs. These peoples were descended from several tribes that migrated to the Caribbean from the South American continent.

The first people that lived in the West Indies were the Ciboneys. Originally from South America, they established themselves first on the island of Trinidad between the years 5500 and 3500 BC. Being excellent navigators, the Ciboneys then migrated to other islands in the West Indies. In the Dominican Republic, the remains of Ciboney sites dating from 2500 BC have been found at Pedernales and Barrera Mordan (near Azua). The Ciboneys were a seminomadic people who lived essentially from hunting, fishing and gathering fruit.

From the time of Christ, successive waves of migrants settled in the Lesser Antilles: the Guapoids from South America (from the 1st to the 4th century), followed by the Saladoids from Central America (from the 4th to the 9th century). These peoples, both Arawak-speaking, lived off the earth: they had advanced tool-making and irrigation techniques, and they produced beautiful pottery which they decorated with drawings. The Gaupoids and the Saladoids soon came in contact with the Ciboneys from the West Indies.

The last people to come to the West Indies from the South American continent were the Caribs from Guyana at the beginning of the 9th century. Expelling the then-resident Arawaks to the Greater Antilles, the Caribs settled mainly in the Lesser Antilles and soon mixed with the already-present Ciboneys creating a new ethnic group called the Tainos. When the Europeans discovered Hispaniola in the 15th century, it was mainly populated by the Tainos.

The Tainos developed a well structured society and an efficient trading system with the other peoples of the Antilles. They generally lived next to the ocean in villages that consisted of about 50 family huts (*bohios*) with 1,000 inhabitants; but the largest villages could have up to 5,000 inhabitants. These villages were part of an empire that was lead by a single ruler called the *cacique*.

Beneath the ruler were three social groups: the nobles who took care of religious functions, the common people and the slaves, who were essential to the economic survival of the empire.

Because they had several food sources, the Tainos were self-sufficient when the Europeans arrived. They grew corn and peppers which they had brought from Mexico, and cassava, also known as manioc, from which they made a bread that served as a staple in their diet. They ate fish, mollusks and wild game, as well as parrots and tiny, voiceless dogs without fur, which were raised by the Tainos strictly for consumption. The Tainos also developed cotton-weaving techniques and created beautiful fabrics. They also made hammocks that became popular with Spanish sailors shortly after the Conquest.

Contrary to popular belief, these island people were not isolated from other peoples in the Americas. The Tainos were great navigators and were familiar with wind and water currents, which allowed them to travel from one island to another. Of all the peoples on the American continent, they seem to have traded the most with native communities in Mexico. The Tainos travelled in canoes that were up to 10m long and could hold 50 sailors. In these ships they sailed as far as Mexico and Venezuela, where they sold cotton fabric.

The Tainos are often considered pacifists, while the Caribs are seen as war-like people, an image that seems to have been based on some distorted observations made by their Spanish conquerors. The Caribs were certainly fierce warriors who conquered Taino villages and violently opposed European settlement on their lands. Moreover, it seems that the Caribs engaged in cannibalistic rituals after defeating their enemies. The Spanish had the impression that the Taino, by comparison, were a peaceful people, when in fact, they too were valiant warriors. This image of the Tainos has persisted: during the European conquest the Taino had a difficult time fending off the Caribs and were ultimately unable to resist the better armed Europeans. The Taino left no descendants; the only remaining native peoples of the West Indies are the Caribs on the island of Dominica.

Little is known about this paleolithic society except that it came into contact with other Arawak peoples around the time of Christ: first the Guapoids (AD 300) and then the Saladoids (between AD 300 and 800). Then around AD 850, a new wave of immigrants, the Caribs, drove the Arawak people from the Lesser Antilles to the Greater Antilles. There the Arawaks mixed with the people already on the islands, particularly on the island of Hispaniola, creating a new ethnic group called the Taïnos.

The island of Hispaniola, except the eastern extremity, which was populated with Caribs, became the adopted homeland of the Tainos. At the time of Columbus' arrival, most of the territory was divided into five distinct kingdoms (Marien, Magua, Jaragua, Maguana and Higüey). Each kingdom was governed by a grand chief, the *cacique*, and included several villages. The rest of the population was divided into three social strata: a group of nobles were in charge of all secular and spiritual ceremonies, while the common people worked the land with the help of slaves. The Tainos depended largely on agriculture for their survival, developing sophisticated irrigation and drainage techniques.

Columbus' first human contacts on the island of Hispaniola were with the Tainos, "Indians" that he judged to be fairly peaceful. Scholars still do not agree on how large the native population of Hispaniola was at the time of the first Spanish explorations. Current estimates put the numbers at around 2 to 3 million individuals. Whatever the numbers, less than 50 years later, in 1535, only a few dozen native families remained on the island. A great many natives died because their immune systems were unable to combat the illnesses brought over by the Europeans. Many also perished in the colonial wars waged by Columbus and his successors. The survivors were then wiped out when the conquistadors imposed forced labour on them.

Christopher Columbus

August 3, 1492, the Genoese navigator Christopher Columbus set sail from the Spanish port of Palos, on an expedition financed by the Catholic kings of Castille and Aragon. Setting out to find a new route to Asia, he sailed westward across the Atlantic Ocean, heading a flotilla of three caravels: The Santa Maria, The Pinta and The Niña.

More than two months later, the expedition landed on an island in the Bahamian archipelago then known by its Taino name, Guanahani. That day, October 12, 1492 marked the official "discovery" of America; Columbus and his men believed they were just off the shores of Southeast Asia.

For several weeks, Columbus explored Guanahani and the neighbouring islands, encountering the natives for the first time. He then headed towards Cuba. After following its shores, the three caravels headed towards another island, known by some natives as Tohio. On the morning of December 6, 1492, this island was "discovered" by Columbus and christened Isla Española (or Hispaniola). Columbus was charmed by the beauty of this large island and wrote about it enthusiastically in his logbook. He sailed slowly along the northern coast, from west to east, making contact with natives and finding them peaceful and welcoming.

The island seemed to Columbus an ideal place to establish the first Spanish colony on the American continent, especially after gold deposits were discovered in some of the rivers.

It was actually the foundering of the Santa Maria that precipitated the settling of this first colony. A fort was built with material salvaged from the wreck. Completed on Christmas Day, 1492, it was christened Fuerte de la Navidad (Nativity Fort). A few weeks later, Columbus left 39 soldiers on the island under the command of Diego de Arana and returned to Spain, where news of his discoveries was received favourably by the Spanish monarchs.

This first Spanish colony on the American continent was soon wiped out. The details of what transpired after Columbus' departure are not known; perhaps the Spanish sailors left on Hispaniola wore out their welcome. One thing is certain: conflict erupted between the two groups, and the natives easily won out.

The Logbook of Christopher Columbus (December 16, 1492)

"May Your Highness believe that these lands are so greatly good and fertile, and especially those of this island of Hispaniola, that there is no one who can tell it; and no one could believe it had he not seen it. And may you believe that this island and all the others are as much yours as Castille; for nothing is lacking except settlement and ordering the Indians to do whatever Your Highness may wish. Because I with the people that I bring with me, who are not many, go about in all these islands without danger; for I have already seen three of these sailors go ashore where there was a crowd of these Indians, and all would flee without the Spaniards wanting to do harm. They do not have arms and they are all naked, and of no skills in arms, and so very cowardly that a thousand would not stand against three. And so they are fit to be ordered about and made to work, plant, and do everything else that may be needed, and build towns and be taught our customs, and to go about clothed."

When Columbus returned 10 months later with 1,500 men, he found no trace of the fort or the 39 soldiers. The explorer then launched the first retaliatory expeditions, which continued for many years and lead to the death of thousands of natives. Columbus later imposed forced labour on the island's inhabitants, and many were even sent to Spain to be sold as slaves. It was thus Christopher Columbus himself who initiated a process that led to the complete extinction of Hispaniola's native population in the decades to come.

The goal of Christopher Columbus' second voyage to America was to found a real Spanish city on Hispaniola. Columbus and his 1,500 men, with supplies, seeds and farm animals, chose a spot not far from the present city of Puerto Plata and founded La Isabela, the first Spanish city in the Americas, in 1493. The city remained the centre of the colony for some time, until it was abandoned due to famines and epidemics.

Gradually, several forts were built closer to the centre of the country to oversee the exploitation of the island's gold deposits. Then, in 1496, Columbus' younger brother

Bartoloméo, founded Santo Domingo, which became the young colony's nerve centre.

In 1500, Christopher Columbus was relieved of his duties as Viceroy of the Indies after Francisco de Bodadilla, appointed by Queen Isabela of Spain to investigate colonial management, accused him of poorly administering the colony, needlessly killing natives and encouraging the slave trade.

Gold and Sugar

During the first quarter century of Spanish colonization, gold mining fuelled Hispaniola's economy. Despite the *encomiendas* system, designed to protect natives from abuse, the island's inhabitants were used as slaves in the gold mines. Living conditions were deplorable, and natives died in such great numbers that the conquistadors eventually had to import slaves from other islands and from Central America.

By 1515, the gold deposits were becoming exhausted and the Spanish began to abandon Hispaniola in favour of other islands and regions in the Americas. Those who remained after the massive exodus of the Spanish population took up farming and stock breeding. On his second voyage to America, Columbus had provided the island with herds of cattle, which quickly grew in number, and crops such as sugar cane, which took well to the local climate. Sugar cane thus became Hispaniola's leading export and the driving force of its economy.

The sugar industry required an abundant workforce, which the island simply did not possess. The Spanish therefore came to depend largely on African slaves, so much so that by the middle of the 16th century, the African population on the island had grown to more than 30,000 individuals.

The sugar boom did not last long, however. During the final decades of the 16th century, the European demand for Dominican sugar cane products began to decline, due in large part to increased exports from Brazil. As a result, the island experienced a second exodus of Spanish colonists.

Sugar cane and cattle nevertheless remained the staples of the economy, but Hispaniola was relegated to a position of marginal importance in the Spanish Empire.

Pirates and Buccaneers

As the Spanish crown lost interest in the island and paid lower and lower prices for Dominican exports, the inhabitants of Hispaniola turned to smugglers to dispose of their merchandise. This angered the Spanish authorities, who decided to regain control of Hispaniola by forcing the Spanish colonists to move to the eastern part of the island, around Santo Domingo, and abandon the rest of the island. This harsh measure was enforced by the Spanish army in 1603 and 1604. The western part of the island was thus completely deserted until several years later, when French buccaneers were drawn to the area. Many settled here permanently and tended the wild cattle that had been left behind. A very profitable business was set up between buccaneers, who slaughtered the animals for leather, and pirates, who transported the leather to Europe.

Although they tried several times, the Spanish authorities never succeeded in putting a stop to the trade. Taking advantage of the buccaneers' presence, France gradually took over this part of the island, which became an official French possession in 1697, with the signing of the Ryswick Treaty.

The eastern part of the island, still under Spanish control, experienced many decades of great economic hardship before finally attaining a certain level of prosperity towards the middle of the 18th century.

The division of Hispaniola between France and Spain led to the birth of the two countries that now share the island: the Dominican Republic and the Republic of Haiti.

Toward Independence

The French Revolution of 1789 had important repercussions even for Hispaniola. In 1791, inspired by the winds of change and the disintegration of France's control, a slave uprising led by Toussaint L'Ouverture broke out in the French colony in the western part of the island.

From the start, the Spanish settlers of Santo Domingo supported the insurgency. However, things changed drastically in 1794, when France abolished slavery in the colony. All of a sudden, Toussaint L'Ouverture's men did an about-face and joined forces with the French to overthrow the Spanish colony on the eastern part of the island. Completely overwhelmed, the Spanish surrendered Santo Domingo to France (1795), which ruled over the whole of Hispaniola for a few years.

In the years that followed, France, under the rule of Napoleon Bonaparte, decided to combat the rising autonomy of Toussaint L'Ouverture's government. A military expedition was sent to Hispaniola in 1802, and L'Ouverture was taken prisoner and brought to France. However, the western part of the island continued to strive for independence from France. In fact, it only became stronger, this time under the leadership of Jean Jacques Desalines. The French forces were soon driven out by the rebels, and on January 1, 1804, the Republic of Haiti was declared.

The French maintained control of the eastern side of the island, but not for long; in 1809, Spanish colonists recaptured Santo Domingo for Spain with the help of British troops at war with Napoleon's France. However, Spanish authorities showed very little interest in the development of this far-off colony, leaving Santo Domingo's settlers little choice but to proclaim their independence in 1821. This independence also proved short-lived, for the Haitian army invaded Santo Domingo the following year. Then, for a period of more than 20 years, until 1844, the Haitians controlled the entire island of Hispaniola.

Haitian domination began to weaken near the end of the 1830s, when an underground Dominican organization began launching attacks on the Haitian army. This organization, known as La Trinitaria, was lead by three men: Juan Pablo Duarte, Ramón Mella and Francisco del Rosario Sanchez. After a few years of fighting, the Haitian army finally retreated, and the eastern half of the island declared itself officially independent. On February 27, 1844, this new nation adopted the name "Dominican Republic".

Years of Uncertainty (1844-1916)

Following the war of independence, La Trinitaria rebels faced opposition from several armed groups within their own country, who wished to take control for themselves. The members of La Trinitaria were quickly defeated at this game, and in September 1844 were completely ousted from power.

A Brief Summary of Dominican History

Near the end of the ice age, nomads from northern Asia began to cross the Bering Strait and populate most of the American continent in successive waves of migration. Later, some migrated to the Caribbean islands.

1492: On his first voyage to the Americas, Christopher Columbus visits several islands, among them Hispaniola, where 39 soldiers stay behind while he returns to Spain.

1493: La Isabela is founded as the first European city in America.

1496: Bartholoméo Columbus, Christopher's brother, founds the city of Santo Domingo.

1535: Less than half a century after the arrival of the conquistadors, the native population on the island has been practically wiped out.

1603-1604: To combat trading between colonists and pirates, Spain forces the colonists to abandon the western regions of the island and resettle in the vicinity of Santo Domingo.

1697: France acquires the western part of the island under the Ryswick Treaty.

1795: French troops take possession of Santo Domingo and occupy it for more than a decade.

1809: Santo Domingo becomes a Spanish colony once again.

1822: The new Republic of Haiti takes over Santo Domingo and occupies it until 1844.

1844: After many years of guerilla fighting, the colonists of Santo Domingo oust the Haitian army. The newly independent nation adopts the name Dominican Republic. After a long period of political instability, the Dominican Republic reverts back to a Spanish colony until 1865.

1916: Already extensively involved in Dominican internal affairs, the United States invades the Dominican Republic, occupying it until 1924.

1930: General Trujillo seizes power by military force and imposes an excessively repressive dicta torship. He remains head of state for more than 30 years, until he is assassinated in May 1961.

1965: The United States sends in troops to prevent Juan Bosch, the legally elected president, from regaining the power he lost earlier at the hands of the military.

1966: Joaquín Balaguer becomes president of the country, and stays in power until 1978. During his 12 years in office, Balaguer often relies on repression as a political tool.

1978: Antonio Guzman, of the Dominican Revolutionary Party (PRD), is elected president. He is replaced in 1982 by Salvador Jorge Blanco, another member of the PRD.

1986: Frustrated by the corruption in Blanco's government, the people re-elect Joaquín Balaguer. The former autocrat is once again re-elected by a very small majority in 1990.

1994: Balaguer is elected once more, amid accusations by the opposition that he has fixed the election results. Under American pressure, Balaguer's term is cut to two years.

1996: Leonel Fernández is brought to power. Dominicans invest much hope in this new government.

Thus began the battle for control, pitting the followers of General Pedro Santana against those of General Buenaventura Baez. For nearly a quarter century, the two military leaders wrestled for power through bloody civil wars. In 1861, General Santana even relinquished control of the Dominican Republic to Spain for a few years.

The Dominicans' string of misfortunes continued when General Ulysses Heureaux became president of the Republic in 1882. He headed a violent dictatorial regime, remaining in power until he was assassinated in 1899. During this time, his poor handling of internal affairs led the country into a series of economic crises.

Upon his death, a succession of governments took power for short periods, creating a period of instability and political chaos that exacerbated the country's economic problems.

It was this situation that precipitated the first of many incursions by the United States into the Dominican political arena. Worried that a European power might take advantage of the economic instability to gain a new foothold in the country, the United States, the new imperialist power that saw Latin America and the Caribbean as its private stomping ground, assumed control of the country's borders and economic affairs.

The American Occupation (1916-1924)

Attempts by the United States to increase their economic control in the Dominican Republic lead to an impasse in November of 1915, when Dominican authorities made it clear that they had no intention of giving in to American pressure. The U.S. reply was prompt: in May of 1916, the United States government ordered the invasion of the Dominican Republic; U.S. Marines quickly took control of Santo Domingo and other major cities. Washington then ordered the dismantling of the Dominican army and the disarmament of the general population.

Under the eight-year American occupation, the Dominican economy was largely remodelled to suit the needs of the United States. For example, as the First World War had made the Americans fear a sugar shortage, the Dominican Republic increased its production of sugar, while the production of other goods needed locally was put aside.

The United States also used this period to eliminate import barriers for American products in the Dominican Republic. The resulting American penetration into the Dominican market forced many small local enterprises out of business. The occupation did have some positive results, however, including an expansion of road and railway networks and an improvement of the educational system.

The American occupation of Dominican territory ended in 1924. In return, the Americans left a semblance of political legitimacy and a powerful National Guard.

The Trujillo Dictatorship

In 1924, Horacio Vasquez won the first free election held in the Dominican Republic. However, this period of democratic rule was short, as General Rafael Leonidas Trujillo (1891-1961), leader of the National Guard, took over the country by military force in 1930 and became the mastermind of one of the darkest periods in Dominican history.

During his "reign", Trujillo, backed by the National Guard and a solid network of spies, imposed an absolute dictatorship with a heinous combination of violence, intimidation, torture, political assassinations and deportations. Under Trujillo, elections were vulgar shams, held only to cover up the excesses of a regime that was nothing less than one of the most terrible dictatorships in the history of the continent.

Trujillo ran things as if they were his personal business. He exercised almost complete control over the development of the Dominican economy by maintaining, either directly or indirectly, a controlling interest in most of the country's industries. Rarely in history has a ruler been as extreme a megalomaniac as Trujillo. Portraits and statues honouring the Generalissimo, who declared himself the nation's "Benefactor", were put up everywhere in the country. In 1936, he even went so far as to change the name of the capital, Santo Domingo, to Ciudad-Trujillo (Trujillo City).

Relations between the Dominican Republic and Haiti were poor during Trujillo's reign. The dictator's rejection of Haiti and its "black" culture were central to Dominican nationalism. Trujillo actually believed that Dominicans had a "civilizing" mission on the island. Relations between the two countries deteriorated even further when, in 1937, under orders from Trujillo, the National Guard massacred between 10,000 and 20,000 Haitians living in the Dominican Republic.

In contrast to the situation between the Dominican Republic and Haiti, Trujillo established excellent relations with the U.S. by offering extremely favourable conditions to American investors and by taking a stand against communism. By the end of the 1950s, maintaining ties with Trujillo became burdensome for the U.S. In Washington, the fear was that the extreme brutality of Trujillo's regime only served to fire up communist revolutionaries in other parts of the continent. Trujillo finally succeeded in completely alienating the Americans in 1960, following the aborted attempt to assassinate Venezuelan president Romulo Bétancourt. From that point on, Trujillo's days were numbered.

This terrible dictatorship, which lasted more than 30 years, ended abruptly on May 30, 1961, when Trujillo was assassinated. At the time of his death, Trujillo was considered one of the 10 richest men in the world, with about 600,000ha of productive farmland to his name and a personal fortune valued at $500 million. The three-decade-long Trujillo regime is estimated to have cost the lives of some 100,000 Dominicans.

The Second American Invasion

After Trujillo's death, the vice-president of the country, Joaquín Balaguer, took over. He soon had to relinquish control to a state council, which organized a presidential election on December 20, 1962. The people elected Juan Bosch of the Dominican Revolutionary Party (PRD). His term did not last long, however; believing that Bosch was determined to re-establish civil liberties, the army ousted him in a coup in September, 1963.

After two years of disastrous economic policies, the increasingly dissatisfied Dominican working classes rose up and, with the help of a dissident army faction, re-established constitutional order on April 24, 1965. Under the pretext that the uprising had been infiltrated by communists, the nervous American government reacted by sending in the marines to assist the Dominican military in putting down the "revolution". Fighting began, causing heavy casualties, and soon the rebels were forced to give in.

A provisional government led by Hector Garcia Godoy was established. Then in a rigged election, one of Trujillo's former comrades-in-arms, Joaquín Balaguer, was elected president in June 1966.

The Contemporary Period

Balaguer led the country for 12 years, winning rigged elections in 1970 and 1974, for which the opposition refused even to put up candidates. During this entire period, Balaguer ruled as an authoritarian, using violence and intimidation to maintain power.

Things took a new turn during the 1978 election, when the Dominican Revolutionary Party (PRD) supported Antonio Guzman in a bid for the presidency. Dominicans were ready for change, yet Balaguer had no intention of relinquishing his control. On election day, when poll results were leaning in favour of Guzman, Balaguer tried to put an end to the vote counting. He almost succeeded, but was forced to give in to outside pressure, mainly from the United States, and admit defeat.

Antonio Guzman remained in power until 1982, but his presidency ended on a tragic note, when he committed suicide upon learning that some of his closest allies had embezzled public funds. After an interim period of a few months, Salvador Jorge Blanco, the new head of the PRD, was elected president and remained so until 1986.

During the presidencies of Guzman and Blanco, many civil liberties were reinstated, which contributed greatly to the popularity of the two men. Unfortunately, with the collapse of sugar markets and the rise in oil prices, the Dominican Republic endured severe economic hardships during this period, leading to deep dissatisfaction among the population. The axe fell on the PRD, when its president, who was also the president of the country, Salvador Jorge Blanco, was personally found guilty of corruption.

In 1986, a disillusioned Dominican electorate facing an unprecedented political void opted to support the former dictator, octogenarian Joaquín Balaguer, in a national election. Balaguer was re-elected in 1990, defeating a disorganized and divided opposition.

Once again, in 1994, he remained in power, not without difficulty, however, and despite accusations that he had fixed the election results in his favour. In a bid to silence critics who questioned the election results and under pressure from the Americans, Balaguer agreed to cut his term to two years and hold another election in 1996. During these last terms, Balaguer governed with a much softer hand than he had previously.

The 1996 election should have belonged to José Francisco Pena Gómez, of the Dominican Revolutionary Party (PRD). Everything indicated he would win, but it was not to be. On the second ballot, a coalition was formed between the Social-Christian Reform Party and the Dominican Liberation Party allowing the latter's candidate, Leonel Fernández, to narrowly defeat Pena Gómez. The results of the election were nevertheless greeted with enthusiasm by the Dominican people, as Fernández offers a real alternative to the Balaguer regime. Quite young (he is in his early 40s) and educated in the United States, Leonel Fernández intends to modernize the country by combatting corruption and investing in health and education.

Politics, Economy and Society

The 500 years that have passed since Columbus' first voyage to America in 1492 have seen an independent Dominican nation emerge. Like most populations in Latin America, Dominicans continue to struggle for real political, economic and social freedom. They must continuously deal with numerous uncertainties that linger over the future of their country. Whatever choices are made in the years to come, the country must first learn to invest in its extraordinarily young population.

Politics

Like the U.S. system, on which it is based, the Dominican legislative system is made up of two chambers, the Senate and the Chamber of Deputies. The Senate has 30 representatives, one for each province in the country and one for the national district; the Chamber of Deputies has 120 members. The president of the country has considerable power;

Simple sun-lit cabins in a picturesque Dominican village, like those seen all over the country.
- *T. Philiptchenko*

"Take the time to take the time".
Philiptchenko

Creole cabin in the shadow of a palm tree.
- *Claude Hervé-Bazin*

he is elected by universal suffrage to a four-year term.

Though there are about twenty political parties, only three play a significant role in the political power play of the country. Up until 1996, the Social-Christian Reform Party (PRSC) (previously called the Reform Party or PR) dominated political life. As leader of the PR and then the PRSC, Joaquín Balaguer was elected president in 1966, 1970 and 1974, then in 1986, 1990 and 1994. The PRSC is the result of the coming-together of the Reform party and the Social-Christian Revolutionary Party.

Founded in Havana (Cuba) by Juan Bosch in 1939, the Dominican Revolutionary Party (PRD) was headed by José Francisco Pena Gómez until recently. In 1973, in-party fighting forced Juan Bosch and his supporters to leave the PRD to found the Dominican Liberation Party. It was as head of the PRD that Juan Bosch was elected president in 1962 before being overthrown by a coup d'état the following year. The PRD was re-elected in 1978 and 1982 with Antonio Guzmán as their leader and then Salvador Jorge Blanco. The most recent election, held in 1996, was won by Leonel Fernández of the Dominican Liberation Party.

In the last few years, Dominican politics have been marked mainly by the growing impatience of the country's working classes, exasperated by the widespread corruption that has reached even the highest levels of government, and by a forced economic austerity plan that has greatly reduced consumer buying power.

Only a few months after his election, Leonel Fernández had to deal with general strikes, which broke out in certain regions of the country. These social ills, which shake things up politically from time to time in the Dominican Republic, are the result of a profound malaise that is particular to many Latin American societies and is linked to the constant growth of the immense gap separating the rich and the poor.

Presently, in the Dominican Republic, while large segments of the society often cannot afford basic foodstuffs and live in humble shacks without running water or electricity, a small minority enjoys fabulous riches and material wealth. This marginalization of a large part of the population is a major stumbling block on the road to true democratization.

As well, until very recently the government of the Dominican Republic stood accused by the international community of participating in the exploitation of Haitian *braceros* (sugar cane cutters). Often surrounded by armed guards, thousands of Haitians had long worked in the fields for a pittance, barely making enough to survive. The Dominican government promised many times to rectify the problem; then, in June 1991, it deported all the illegal workers back to Haiti.

Many Haitians have nevertheless remained in the country, usually working at menial, low-paying jobs in the construction or agricultural sectors. Working conditions remain unbearable on sugar plantations, and, generally, the situation of Haitians living in the Dominican Republic is still a problem. The country's new president, Leonel Fernández, seems to show much more goodwill than his predecessor.

A meeting with his Haitian counterpart at the end of 1996 lead to an agreement concerning the wages paid to cane-cutters.

The Economy

The Dominican economy has become somewhat more modern and diverse in recent decades, but farming and raising livestock are still central activities. More than 40% of the country's total surface area serves as pasture for cattle, and approximately one third is used for growing food for human consumption. Contrary to the situation in many Caribbean countries, most of the dietary staples consumed on the island are produced locally.

Sugar cane, which was introduced to the island by Columbus, is still the largest crop in the country. Its cultivation requires a large work force, and refined cane sugar is the country's primary agricultural export.

Among the other commodities exported by the Dominican Republic, the most important are tobacco, cocoa, coffee, rice and various tropical fruits. Dairy production and the breeding of cattle, pigs and poultry serve mainly to satisfy local demand.

Coffee Plant

The Dominican Republic is rich in mineral resources, though many are still largely untapped. The only large-scale mining operations focus on silver, gold, nickel and iron. In recent years, nickel has come to occupy an important place on the foreign markets. In terms of value, it is presently the most import ant export. The Dominican Republic also produces large quantities of salt, which is extracted primarily from deposits along the shores of Lago Enriquillo. In addition, hydroelectric facilities produce about 20% of the country's energy requirements. As with most Caribbean countries, the Dominican Republic is still largely dependent on foreign imports for energy.

Despite recent efforts to diversify industrial production, sugar cane refinement is still the biggest Dominican industry. Sugar cane is used mainly to produce raw sugar, and secondarily for rum and molasses.

Labour-intensive light industries, such as the production of textiles, shoes, clothing and food products, have grown steadily in the last few decades. The Dominican Republic's heavy industries are mostly in the plastic, metallurgy and oil refining sectors.

The Dominican government continues to favour the development of industrial zones near several large cities for the use of foreign businesses. As a consequence, many companies, mostly American, Canadian and Asian ones, now assemble their products in the Dominican Republic, thus taking advantage of a cheap labour force.

Tourism is also one of the mainstays of the economy; it is now the major source of foreign currency in the country. Though largely dominated by companies not owned by Dominican interests, tourism directly employs close to 200,000 people Realizing the economic importance of tourism with respect to the development of the country, the new government has increased its support for this sector. The tourism industry is nonetheless a key sector of the Dominican economy and contributes about 70% to the gross national product.

Tourism began to develop in the 1980s, and since then the Dominican Republic has marketed itself as an inexpensive sun destination. Thanks to local production of most of the necessary foodstuffs, many hotel complexes are able to offer "all-inclusive" packages (room, meals and drinks) at very competitive rates compared to what is offered in other islands in the region.

Finally, the country's continued dependence on sugar markets constitutes a recurring problem for the structure of the national economy. The economic crisis that has plagued the Dominican Republic for over 10 years is tied to a reduction in American sugar imports and the resulting sharp drop in the price of sugar. The Dominican Republic also has a considerable foreign debt, which seems out of control, further hindering the country's economic development. The employment situation is just as dismal, with more than a quarter of the potential workforce left idle.

Population

Covering two thirds of the island of Hispaniola, which it shares with Haiti, the Dominican Republic has a population of 7,900,000, according to the most recent census. A majority of Dominicans live in either Santo Domingo or the Cibao valley. The population density in the country has reached 150 inhabitants per square kilometre, and the birth rate is among the highest in the Caribbean. Presently, 48% of Dominicans are under 14 years old. The poor economic conditions in recent years have pushed the number of Dominicans emigrating to Puerto Rico to as many as 500 per week.

Although it is difficult to present a precise picture of the Dominican Republic's racial composition, there are three main population groups in the country: mulattos make up about 75% of the population, while whites and blacks represent 15% and 10%, respectively. A marked economic disparity exists between whites and blacks, generally favouring whites.

The origins of the Dominican population are diverse, but most have Spanish or African backgrounds. A smaller percentage, typically working at lower-paying jobs, are of Haitian descent. Generally speaking, citizens of Haitian origin are poorly accepted; the conflicts that have marked relations between the two countries are not soon forgotten.

In addition, the country's large urban centres often have small Asian communities, while a number of the residents of Sosúa are descendants of Eastern European Jews who escaped Nazi Germany in the 1930s. There are no descendants of the indigenous peoples that once inhabited the island of Hispaniola; this group was completely wiped out at the beginning of colonization.

More than 95% of Dominicans consider themselves Catholic, while a small number of people, most of whom live in mountainous areas, practise voodoo.

The official language of the Dominican Republic, and the mother tongue of 95% of the population, is Spanish. Along the Haitian border a few people speak Creole. Throughout the country, even in tourist areas, visitors will be addressed in Spanish, though many people speak English and French as well.

Culture, Traditions and Lifestyle

The Dominican Republic was a Spanish colony for many years during which time it absorbed thousands of African immigrants. The artistic activity on the island has been shaped by these two cultures. During the early years of colonization, the arts flourished, especially in the 16th century. It was not until the 19th century, when the country gained independence and a certain stability, that artistic expression began to develop. From the end of the 19th century to the present, the arts have thrived continually. Unfortunately, censorship has often thrived as well.

Literature

The first writer to document the charms of Hispaniola was none other than Christopher Columbus; his log books provide the first descriptions of the region. Very early in the country's colonial history, Dominican writers emerged with a style of their own. The **Santo Tomas de Aquino University**, founded in 1538, was central to the development of this literature. The earliest Dominican works consist essentially of essays, journals and chronicles written by the first explorers and missionaries, and aim mainly to describe the territory and spread knowledge of its existence. Among the first texts of note are *The Historia Natural y General de Indias* by Gonzalo Fernandez de Oviedo, *Doctrina Cristina* by Brother Pedro de Cordoba, and *Historia de las Indias* by Brother Bartoloméo de las Casas.

The French invasion and the difficulties with Spain in the 17th and 18th centuries slowed the literary development of the country. Dominican literature did not enjoy a resurgence until the 19th century. Several influential writers emerged during that period, most notably Felix Maria del Monte, known for his patriotic poetry. The texts of Salomé Ureña, advocating an improvement in conditions for women on the island, are also significant. *Enriquillo*, a historical text written by Manuel de Jesus Galvan in the late 19th and early 20th centuries, also ranks among the most important works of the time.

The period immediately following the country's independence (1880), though marred by the American invasion (1916), saw the development of a literature that emphasized an awareness of social realities, as well as more patriotic writings. It was in this context that Federico Bermúdez wrote *Los Humildes*, denouncing the suffering of the Dominican people.

Federico Garcia Godoy recounts the advent of independence in three powerful short stories: *Rufinito*, *Alma Dominicana*, and *Guanuma*. Though fairly conservative in his choice of subjects, Gaston Fernando Deligne is a master of the Spanish language and one of the country's most important poets. Another writer by the name of Domingo Moreno Jimines headed a group that sang the praises of the good and simple values of peasant life.

Later, during the dictatorship of President Trujillo, literary activity slowed down. In a climate of brutal repression, Dominican authors had much less freedom of expression. Writers such as Manuel Rueda and Lupo Fernandez Rueda used symbols and metaphors to covertly protest certain aspects of the political regime. Others were forced into exile. It was in such a context, while in Cuba, that Pedro Mir wrote his beautiful poem *Hay un país en el Mundo*.

During the 1940s, a greater openness toward foreign literary movements led to the emergence of the "surprise" poetry movement. Among the so-called "independent" poets, Tomas Hernandez Franco became known for his modern works, which protested the existing regime. Works with wider appeal were also created during this period.

Antonio Fernandez Spencer published collections of poetry that gained international recognition. One of the most important authors of the 20th century, Juan Bosch, did most of his writing during the Trujillo dictatorship. His engaging, beautifully written essays describe the daily life of Dominican peasants. After the fall of the Trujillo regime, Bosch led the Dominican Republic for a few months, and remained an important political figure for many years. However, during the 30 years of Trujillo, many authors opted for silence or exile, publishing their texts only after Trujillo's death in 1961. Despite these difficult years, Dominican literary movements remained dynamic and innovative.

Literary expression has since been granted more and more freedom and several authors, often influenced by foreign literary trends, stand out for the quality of their work. The most important are Ivan Garcia Guerra, Miguel Alfonseca, Jeannette Miller, Alexis Gómez and Soledad Álvarez and the former president of the country, Joaquín Balaguer.

Painting

The Dominican Republic has been and is home to numerous talented painters who have gained renown in Dominican and international artistic circles. Usually vibrantly coloured and buoyant, local painting is quite emblematic of the artistic intensity of the island. Among the distinguished artists of the country are Guillo Pérez, Elsa Núñez, Fernando Ureña Rib, Candido Bibo and Manuel Severino. Two celebrated painters in particular, Giorgi Morel and Jaime Colsón, stand out among the country's masters.

Music and Dance

Music and dance occupy a very important place in the cultural landscape of the Dominican Republic. Much more than an occasional pastime, music accompanies every part of a Dominican day, whether it be on a crowded bus, in the most humble of market stalls, at work, at home, or late at night in the nightclubs of Santo Domingo and other cities.

Among the current musical trends, a Dominican favourite is the *merengue*, that rousing, furiously rhythmic music that has its origins on the island. Though originally identified with the rural classes, the popularity of the *merengue* cuts through the various social divisions of the country. It was in the Dominican countryside that this accordion, tambourine, saxophone and drum music, with its son rhythm, was conceived.

The *merengue* became fashionable throughout the

country in the 1930s, under the regime of General Trujillo, who was a true fan of this music. The talented artist Francisco Uloa made a name for himself during this period. At the end of the 1950s, the major groups had their turn at fame, most notably Johnny Ventura. Since then, while conserving its original rhythms, the *merengue* has been developed: leaving more space for the saxophone; replacing the accordion with an electric guitar and the piano with a synthesizer. Contemporary *merengue* has also been influenced by various other styles, such as salsa, rock, zook and reggae.

Among the other Dominican *merengue* stars we should mention Tonio Rosario and Fernandito Villalona.

Although the Dominicans adore *merengue*, they also appreciate *batchata*, their other national music. The *batchata* is becoming more popular among most of the social classes of the Dominican Republic. This music, with rhythms slower than *merengue*, has traditionally been associated with Dominican workers and peasants. Love remains the essential theme that colours the songs of *batchata* singers. Currently, the popular artists of the country are Antony Santos, Raúl Rodríguez and Luis Vargas.

For a while now, the appeal of *merengue* has extended beyond the borders of the Dominican Republic. Some of the country's greatest talents have become international stars, as well known the world over as they are throughout the Caribbean and in other Spanish-speaking countries. In the 1980s, the group 4:40 and its leader Juan Luís Guerra were a huge success on the international scene.

Though Dominicans adore *merengue*, which they consider their national music, they are also very fond of other types of music. Spanish and Latin-American singers are common and very well-liked with locals. North American "top-40" music, as well as Afro-American and Caribbean movements, such as reggae, are also prevalent in the country. Classical music enjoys a following here as well. Santo Domingo even has its own reputed symphony orchestra.

Baseball

Baseball is at least as popular in the Dominican Republic as it is in the United States, where it originated. Young Dominicans practise this sport more than any other; there are baseball fields in every neighbourhood in the capital and every village of the country. And with equipment requirements limited to a glove, a ball and a bat, it is very economical to play, a definite plus in a country where money is an issue for the majority of the population.

Baseball is the national sport of Dominicans, and is also a very popular pastime. The exploits of the big Dominican stars of professional baseball are followed passionately and reported upon at length in the local media.

Professional baseball has existed in the Dominican Republic for more than 100 years. The professional league currently numbers five teams, two in Santo Domingo and the others in San Pedro de Macoris, Santiago de los Caballeros and La Romana.

Each team plays about 60 games between the months of October and February, and the season ends with a championship series between the best teams in the Caribbean.

Discussions are currently underway to grant Puerto Plata its very own professional team. There is talk of completely renovating the old stadium at the entrance to the city (near The Brugal Rum Distillery), in order to accommodate a Puerto Plata team that could prove to be very popular with tourists.

The reputation of Dominican baseball grew in the 1950s following the successes of the first Dominicans to play in the majors. In 1956, Ozzie Virgil became the first player to make a name for himself in the United States. But it was thanks to the remarkable talent of right-handed pitcher Juan Marichal, signed by the San Francisco Giants and of the Alou brothers (Felipe, Mateo, Moïse and Jesús) that the quality of Dominican players became known.

Since Virgil, Marichal and the Alou brothers, more than 200 young Dominicans have stepped up to the plate in the major leagues.

Some of the more noteworthy players include Rico Carty, Manny Mota, César Cedeno, Pedro Guerrero, Frank Taveras, Pepe Fria, Alfredo Griffín, Rafael Landestoy, Joaquín Andujar, Tony Pena, George Bell, Damaso García, Pasqual Pérez, Mario Soto, Raul Mondesi, Julio Franco, Vladimir Guerrero, Moises Alou, Mel Rojas, Carlos Pérez and Sammy Sosa. After the United States, the Dominican Republic that has produced the most major league players. The city of San Pedro Macoris actually claims to have spawned more players *per capita* than any other city in the world.

Cockfighting

Introduced by the Spanish, cockfights are held all over the Dominican Republic. Men gather around the "pits" (packed-dirt arenas) to watch and cheer on a battle between two cocks.

Beforehand, there is a ceremony, during which the cocks are weighed and fitted with spurs, and their owners are introduced. Then, once the judges have decided that the birds qualify, the fight begins. Victory goes to the cock left breathing at the end.

Practical Information

Whether alone or in a group, it is easy to travel anywhere in the Dominican Republic, especially on the north coast.

In order to make the most of your stay, it is important to be well prepared. In addition to providing information on local customs, this chapter is intended to help you plan your trip.

Entrance Formalities

Make sure you bring all the necessary papers to enter and exit the country. Though requirements are not very strict, you will need certain documents to travel in the Dominican Republic. You should therefore keep your important papers safe at all times.

Passport

To enter the Dominican Republic, citizens of Canada, the United States and the European Union are advised to bring their passport, making sure it is valid for the length of their stay. It is also possible to enter the country with an official birth certificate or a citizenship card accompanied by an identification card and a photograph.

Be aware though, that in case of problems with the authorities, the most official proof of your identity is your passport.

It is a good idea to keep a photocopy of the key pages of your passport, and to write down your passport number and its expiry date. This way, in case the document is lost or stolen, it will be much easier to replace (do the same with your birth certificate or citizenship card). If this should occur, contact your country's consulate or embassy to have a new one issued.

Tourist Card

To enter the country, all visitors are required to have a tourist card (*tarjeta del tourista*) which is valid for 60 days. In most cases, the card is issued by a travel agent, at the airport, or on the airplane with the plane ticket. The price of your airline ticket or package will usually include the cost of the card, which is about $10. Keep it in a safe place during your stay, as it must be returned to authorities upon departure.

Visas

A visa is not required for visitors from Canada, the United States, and the European community. Citizens of other countries must contact the closest embassy or consulate of the Dominican Republic to obtain a visa.

Departure Tax

Each person leaving the Dominican Republic must pay a departure tax of $10. The tax is collected at the airport when you check in for your return flight. Remember to keep this amount in cash, as credit cards are not accepted.

Customs

Visitors may enter the country with up to one litre of alcohol, 200 cigarettes and up to $100 worth of goods (not counting personal belongings). Bringing in illegal drugs and firearms is, of course, prohibited.

Embassies and Consulates

Embassies and consulates can be an invaluable source of help to visitors who find themselves in trouble. For example, consulates can provide names of doctors or lawyers in the case of death or serious injury. However, only urgent cases are handled. The cost of these services is not covered by the consulates. The following diplomatic missions are in Santo Domingo:

Belgium Agencias
Navieras Báez
504 av. Abraham Lincoln
☎ *(809) 562-1661*
⇌ *(809) 562-3383*

Canada
30 Avenida Máximo Gomez
☎ *(809) 685-1136*
⇌ *(809) 682-2691*

Denmark
504 Abraham Lincoln
☎ *(809) 549-5100*

Finland
77 M.H. Urena
☎ *(809) 549-4420*

Germany
37 Calle Lic. Juan Tomás Mejía y Cotes
Apartado Postal 1235
☎ *(809) 565-8811*
☎ *(809) 565-8812*

Great Britain
Saint George School 552 Av. Abraham Lincoln
☎ *(809) 562-5015*
or
Apartado Postal 30341
Av. Romulo Betancourt # 1302
apt. 202
☎ *(809) 532-4216*

Italy
4 Rodriguez Obijo
☎ *(809) 689-3684*

Netherlands
Mayor Enrique Valverde
☎ *(809) 565-5240*

Spain
1205 Independencia
☎ *(809) 535-1615*

Sweden
31 Maximo Gomez
☎ *(809) 685-2131*

Switzerland
26, av. José Gabria García
☎ *(809) 685-0126.*

United States
At the corner of Calle Cesar Nicolas Pension and Calle Leopold Navarro
☎ *(809) 541-2171*

Dominican Embassies and Consulates Abroad

Belgium
160-A av. Louise
1050 Bruxelles
☎ *648-0840*
⇌ *640-9561*

Canada
1650 de Maisonneuve West, Suite 302
Montreal, Quebec
☎ *(514) 933-9008*
☎ *1-800-563-1611*

Germany
Burgstrasse # 87
5300 Bonn, 2nd floor
Germany
☎ *00228-36-4956*

Practical Information

Spain
José Mª Escuza n°20, 6A, 48013
Bilbao
☎/⇌ *34.4.427.63.88*

Switzerland
16 rue Genus, Genève
☎ *738-0018*

United States
1715 22nd St. N.W., Washington, D.C.
20008, U.S.A.
☎ *(202) 332-6280*
or
1501 Broadway, 4th floor, New York
N.Y. 10036, U.S.A.
☎ *(212) 768-2480*
or
1038 Brickell Ave., Miami, FLA
33131, U.S.A.
☎ *(305) 358-3221*
or
870 Market St., Suite 915, San Francisco, CA, 94102, U.S.A.
☎ *(415) 783-7530*

Tourist Offices

These offices help travellers plan their trips to the Dominican Republic. Their personnel can answer questions and provide you with brochures.

Belgium
Ave. Louise, No. 271, 8è étage, 1050
Bruxelles
☎ *(322) 646-1300*
⇌ *(322) 649-3962*

Canada
2080 Crescent,
Montreal, Quebec
H3G 2V8
☎ *(514) 499-1918*
⇌ *(514) 499-1393*
or
35 Church Street, Unit 53
Toronto, Ontario
M5E 1T3
☎ *(416) 361-2126*
or *1-888-494-5050*
⇌ *(416) 361-2130*

Germany
Hochstrasse 17, D-60313, Frankfurt
☎ *4969-9139-7878*
⇌ *4969-283430*

Great Britain
1 Hay Hill, Berkely Square
London W1X 7LF
☎ *(171) 495-4322*
⇌ *(171) 491-8689*

Italy
Piazza Castello 25
20121 Milano, Italia
☎ *(392) 805-7781*
⇌ *(392) 865-861*

United States
136 East 57th Street, Suite 803
New York, N.Y., 10022
☎ *(212) 588-1012/13/14*
⇌ *(212) 588-1015*
or
2355 Salzedo St., Suite 307, Coral
Gables, Miami, Fla., 33134
☎ *(305) 444-4592*
⇌ *(305) 444-4845*
or
561 West Diversey Bldg, Suite 214
Chicago, IL
60614-1643
☎ *(773) 529-1336*
☎ *1-888-303-1336*
⇌ *(773) 529-1338*

Tourist Information in the Dominican Republic

Secretaria de Estado de Turismo
Oficinas Gubernamentales
Block D, Mexico Ave.
at the corner of Calle 30 de Marzo
Suite 497, Santo Domingo
☎ *(809) 221-4660*
⇌ *(809) 682-3806*

Tourist Information
1, Avenida Hermanas Mirabel
Parque Costeroé, Puerto Plata
☎ *586-3676*
⇌ *586-5169*

On the Internet

www.dominican.com.do

Entering the Country

Several tour operators offer packages including accommodation, meals and airfare on a charter flight. These "all-inclusive" deals generally bring visitors to tourist villages like Playa Dorada, Sosúa or Cabarete. Check with your travel agent to find out which packages are available.

It is also easy to head off with just an airline ticket and to find accommodation on location, due to the abundance of hotels situated in all regions of the island. The advantage of this type of travel is that you will see much more of the island and can choose where to stay each day. Except during peak travel times (Christmas vacation and the Easter week), you should not have any trouble finding accommodation without reservations, either in out-of-the-way Dominican villages (if you don't require the utmost in comfort) or in the popular resorts.

By Plane

The Dominican Republic has seven international airports which are located in Santo Domingo (Las Américas and Herreras), Puerto Plata, Punta Cana, La Romana (Cajuiles) and Barahona. The most important airports are in Santo Domingo and Puerto Plata.

Puerto Plata International Airport

The Puerto Plata International Airport has expansive, full-service facilities. Several boutiques sell local products here, though at prices slightly higher than in the city.

Puerto Plata International Airport

Located 18km east of Puerto Plata
☎ *586-0219*

Domestic Flights

Air Santo Domingo
(☎ *683-8020*) connects the main cities of the country.

Taxis

A taxi from the airport costs around $14 to Puerto Plata, $7 to Sosúa and $20 to Cabarete. A considerable number of taxis wait outside the airport.

Insurance

Health Insurance

Health insurance is the most important type of insurance for travellers and should be purchased before your departure. A comprehensive health insurance policy that provides a level of coverage sufficient to pay for hospitalization, nursing care and doctor's fees is recommended. Keep in mind that health care costs are rising quickly everywhere. The policy should also have a repatriation clause in case the required care is not available in the Dominican Republic. As patients are sometimes asked to pay for medical services up front, find out what provisions your policy makes in this case. Always carry your health insurance policy with you when travelling to avoid problems if you are in an accident, and get receipts for any expenses incurred.

Theft Insurance

Most residential insurance policies in North America protect some of your goods from theft, even if the theft occurs in a foreign country. To make a claim, you must fill out a police report. Usually the coverage for a theft abroad is 10% of your total coverage. If you plan to travel with valuable objects, check your policy or with an insurance agency to see if additional baggage insurance is necessary. European visitors should take out baggage insurance.

Cancellation Insurance

This type of insurance is usually offered by your travel agent when you purchase your air ticket or tour package. It covers any non-refundable payments to travel suppliers such as airlines, and must be purchased at the same time as initial payment is made for air tickets or tour packages. This insurance allows you to be reimbursed for the ticket or package deal if your trip must be cancelled due to serious illness or death. This type of insurance can be useful, but weigh the likelihood of your using it against the price.

Health

The Dominican Republic is a wonderful country to explore; however, travellers should be aware of and protect themselves against a number of health risks associated with the region, such as malaria, typhoid, diphtheria, tetanus, polio and hepatitis A. Travellers are advised to consult a doctor (or travellers' clinic) for advice on what precautions to take. Remember that it is much easier to prevent these illnesses than it is to cure them. It is thus worthwhile to take the recommended medications, vaccinations and precautions in order to avoid any health problems.

Illnesses

This section is intended to give a brief introduction to some of the more common illnesses found in the country, and thus should be used for information purposes only.

Malaria

Malaria (or paludism) is caused by a parasite in the blood called *Plasmodium sp*. This parasite is transmitted by anopheles mosquitoes, which bite from nightfall until dawn. In the Dominican Republic, the rural and urban zones of the whole country, especially along the Haitian border, can sometimes be hot-spots. The risk is minimal and anti-malaria drugs are not necessary for short stays in resort areas. It is nevertheless a good idea to take measures to prevent mosquito bites (see p 52).

The symptoms of malaria include high fever, chills, extreme fatigue and headaches, as well as stomach and muscle aches. There are several forms of malaria, including one serious type caused by *P. falciparum*. The disease can take hold while you are still on holiday or up to 12 weeks following your return; in some cases the symptoms can appear months later.

Hepatitis A

This disease is generally transmitted by ingesting food or water that has been contaminated by faecal matter. The symptoms include fever, yellowing of the skin, loss of appetite and fatigue, and can appear between 15 and 50 days after infection. An effective vaccination by injection is available. Besides the recommended vaccine, good hygiene is important. Always wash your hands before every meal, and ensure that the food and preparation area are clean.

Hepatits B

Hepatitis B, like hepatitis A, affects the liver, but is transmitted through direct contact with body fluids. The symptoms are flu-like, and similar to those of hepatitis A. A vaccination exists but must be administered over an extended period of time, so be sure to check with your doctor several weeks in advance.

Dengue

Also called "breakbone fever", Dengue is transmitted by mosquitoes. In its most benign form it can cause flu-like symptoms such as headaches, chills and sweating, aching muscles and nausea. In its haemorrhagic form, the most serious and rarest form, it can be fatal. There is no vaccine for the virus, so take the usual precautions to avoid mosquito bites.

Typhoid Fever

This illness is caused by ingesting food that has come in contact (direct or indirect) with an infected person's stool. Common symptoms include high fever, loss of appetite, headaches, constipation and occasionally diarrhea, as well as the appearance of red spots on the skin. These symptoms will appear one to three weeks after infection. The type of vaccination you get (it exists in two forms, oral and by injection) will depend on your trip. Once again, it is always a good idea to visit a travellers' clinic a few weeks before your departure.

Diphtheria and Tetanus

These two illnesses, against which most people are vaccinated during their childhood, can have serious consequences. Before leaving, check that your vaccinations are valid; you may need a booster shot. Diphtheria is a bacterial infection that is transmitted by nose and throat secretions or by skin lesions on an infected person. Symptoms include sore throat, high fever, general aches and pains and occasionally skin infections.

Tetanus is caused by a bacteria that enters your body through an open wound that comes in contact with contaminated dust or rusty metal.

Other Health Tips

Cases of illnesses like AIDS and certain venereal diseases have been reported; it is therefore a good idea to be careful.

Near the villages of Hato Mayor, Higüey, Nisibon and El Seibo, fresh water is often contaminated by an organism that causes schistosomiasis. This infection, which is caused by a parasite entering the body and attacking the liver and nervous system, is difficult to treat. It is therefore best to avoid swimming in fresh water.

Remember that consuming too much alcohol, particularly during prolonged exposure to the sun, can cause severe dehydration and lead to health problems.

Due to a lack of financial resources, Dominican medical facilities may not be as up-to-date as those in your own country. Therefore, if you need medical services, expect them to be different from what you are used to. The clinics outside large urban centres might more seem modest. In general, however, clinics are better equipped than hospitals, so head to a clinic first. In tourist areas, there are always doctors who can speak English. Before a blood transfusion, be sure that quality control tests have been carried out on the blood.

Insufficiently treated water, which can contain harmful bacteria, is the cause of most of the health problems travellers are likely to encounter, such as stomach upset, diarrhea or fever. Throughout the country, it is a good idea to drink bottled water (when buying bottled water, make sure the bottle is properly sealed), or to purify your own with iodine or a water purifier. Most major hotels treat their water, but always ask before you drink.

Ice cubes should be avoided, as they may be made of contaminated water. In addition, fresh fruits and vegetables that have been washed but not peeled can also pose a health risk. Make sure that the vegetables you eat are well-cooked and peel your own fruit. Do not eat lettuce, unless it has been hydroponically grown (some vegetarian restaurants serve this type of lettuce; ask). Remember: cook it, peel it or forget it.

If you do get diarrhea, soothe your stomach by avoiding solids; instead, drink carbonated beverages, bottled water, or weak tea (avoid milk) until you recover. As dehydration can be dangerous, drinking sufficient quantities of liquid is crucial. Pharmacies sell various preparations for the treatment of diarrhea, with different effects.

Oral rehydration products will replace the minerals and electrolytes that your body has lost as a result of the diarrhea. In a pinch, you can make your own rehydration solution by mixing one litre of pure water with one teaspoon of sugar and two or three teaspoons of salt. After, eat easily digestible foods like rice to give your stomach time to adjust. If symptoms become more serious (high fever, persistent diarrhea), see a doctor as antibiotics may be necessary.

Food and climate can also cause problems. Pay attention to food's freshness, and the cleanliness of the preparation area. Good hygiene (wash your hands often) will help avoid undesirable situations.

It is best not to walk around barefoot as parasites and insects can cause a variety of problems, the least of which is athlete's foot.

Mosquitoes

A nuisance common to many countries, mosquitoes are no strangers to the Dominican Republic. They are particularly numerous during the rainy season (May to October). Protect yourself with a good insect repellent. Repellents with DEET are the most effective. The concentration of DEET varies from one product to the next; the higher the concentration, the longer the protection.

In rare cases, the use of repellents with high concentrations (35% or more) of DEET has been associated with convulsions in young children; it is therefore important to apply these products sparingly, on exposed surfaces, and to wash it off once back inside. A concentration of 35% DEET will protect for four to six hours, while 95% will last from 10 to 12hrs. New formulas with DEET in lesser concentrations, but which last just as long, are available.

To further reduce the possibility of getting bitten, do not wear perfume or bright colours. Sundown is an especially active time for insects. When walking in wooded areas, cover your legs and ankles well. Insect coils can help provide a better night's sleep. Before bed, apply insect repellent to your skin and to the headboard and baseboard of your bed. If possible, get an air-conditioned room, or bring a mosquito net.

Lastly, since it is impossible to completely avoid contact with mosquitoes, bring along a cream to soothe the bites you will invariably get.

The Sun

Its benefits are many, but so are its harms. Always wear sunscreen (SPF 15 for adults and SPF 30 for children) and apply it 20 to 30mins before exposure. Many creams on the market do not offer adequate protection; ask a pharmacist. Too much sun can cause sunstroke (dizziness, vomiting, fever, etc.). Be careful, especially the first few days, as it takes time to get used to the sun. Take sun in small doses and protect yourself with a hat and sunglasses.

First-Aid Kit

A small first-aid kit can be very useful. Bring along sufficient amounts of any medications you take regularly as well as a valid prescription in case you lose your supply of them. It can be difficult to find certain medications in small towns in the Dominican Republic. Other medications such as anti-malaria pills and Imodium (or an equivalent), can also be hard to find. Finally, do not forget self-adhesive bandages, disinfectant cream or ointment, analgesics (pain-killers), antihistamines (for allergies), an extra pair of sunglasses or contact lenses, contact lens solution, and medicine for upset stomach. Though these items are all available in the Dominican Republic, they might be difficult to find in remote villages.

Climate

There are two seasons in the Dominican Republic: the cool season (from November to April) and the rainy season (from May to October). The cool season is the most pleasant, as the heat is less stifling, the rain less frequent and the humidity lower. Temperatures hover around 29°C during the day and dip to about 19°C at night.

During the rainy season, showers are heavy but short, so it is still possible to travel. Rain is most frequent from May to mid-June. During the rainy season, the average temperature is 31°C during the day and 22°C at night. The number of hours of daylight remains fairly constant throughout the year. Hurricanes, though rare, occur during the rainy season.

Packing

The type of clothing required does not vary much from season to season. In general, loose-fitting, comfortable cotton or linen clothes are best. When exploring urban areas, wear closed shoes that cover the entire foot rather than sandals, as they will protect against cuts that could become infected. Bring a sweater or long-sleeved shirt for cool evenings, and rubber sandals (thongs or flip-flops) to wear at the beach and in the shower. During the rainy season, an umbrella is useful for staying dry during brief tropical showers. To visit certain attractions such as churches, you must wear a skirt that covers the knees or long pants. For evenings out, you might need more formal clothes, as a number of places have dress codes. Finally, if you expect to go hiking in the mountains, bring along some good hiking boots and a sweater.

Safety and Security

Although the Dominican Republic is not a dangerous country, it has its share of thieves, particularly in the resort towns and in Santo Domingo. Keep in mind that to the majority of people in the country, some of your possessions (things like cameras, leather suitcases, video cameras, and jewellery) represent a great deal of money, especially when you consider that the minimum monthly salary is 3,800 pesos (*$250*).

A degree of caution can help avoid problems. For example, do not wear too much jewellery, keep your electronic equipment in a nondescript shoulder bag slung across your chest, and avoid revealing the contents of your wallet when paying for something. Be doubly careful at night, and stay away from dark streets, especially if there are strangers lurking about. Finally, some neighbourhoods of Santo Domingo – around the Puente Duarte and behind Calle Mella, for example – should be avoided, particularly at night. To be safe, do not wander into an area you know nothing about.

A money belt can be used to conceal cash under your clothes, traveller's cheques and your passport. If your bags should happen to be stolen, you will at least have the money and documents necessary to get by. Remember that the less attention you draw to yourself, the less chance you have of being robbed.

If you bring valuables to the beach, you are strongly recommended to keep a constant eye on them. It is best to keep your valuables in the small safes available at most hotels.

In a case of an emergency, dial **911**.

Transportation

By Car

General Orientation

Highway 5 links the coastal cities from Puerto Plata to the Samaná Peninsula. Most of the road is in excellent condition. Several roads branch off of Highway 5 and head across the magnificent Cordillera Septentrionale toward the centre of the country. One of the most picturesque and useful is the **Carretera Turistica**, which provides a quick link between Santiago de los Caballeros and the coast. The advantage of this lovely mountain road is that trucks are not allowed on it, so traffic is faster and more pleasant.

The roads on the Atlantic coast are generally in good condition and have little traffic. This changes dramatically around Puerto Plata, however, where the road widens to include as many as four lanes. Many of the motorists take advantage of the situation, and accelerate their speed in an attempt to bypass – sometimes in a somewhat reckless way – mopeds and other slower vehicles. Caution is advised, especially during the morning and late-afternoon rush hours, if you would like to avoid getting flustered by a rash vehicle coming out of nowhere to cut you off.

Distances can be long in the Dominican Republic, especially since the roads, though generally in good condition, often pass through small villages where drivers must slow down. Furthermore, very few roads have passing lanes, and the condition of some of the smaller roads makes it difficult to drive faster than 40 kph. Thus, it is important to plan your itinerary carefully.

Puerto Plata

There is only one main road into Puerto Plata. It crosses the city from west to east, where it becomes Avenida Circunvalación Sur. Running parallel, Avenida Circunvalación Norte (which becomes Avenida Luperón) follows the ocean from Long Beach to the San Felipe Fortress.

These two main roads are linked to the west by Avenida Colón and to the east by Avenida Mirabal. The four avenues form a rectangle around the city, making it easy to find your way around. Most of the hotels in Puerto Plata are located on the east side of town, facing Long Beach, or along Avenida Mirabal.

If you haven't got a car, it is easy to get around by hailing a motorcycle, locals are used to picking up passengers and will take you from one end of the city to the other for about $1.

Renting a Car

Renting a car in the Dominican Republic is easy, as most of the large companies have offices in the country. It will cost an average of $50 a day (unlimited mileage) for a compact car, not including insurance and taxes. The minimum age for renting a car is 25, and you must possess have credit card. Choose a vehicle that is in good condition, preferably a new one. A few local companies offer low prices, but their cars are often in poor condition, and they do not offer much assistance in case of breakdown. Therefore, before heading off on a long journey, choose your car carefully.

It is strongly recommended that you take out sufficient automobile insurance to cover all costs in case of an accident. A $700 deductible is fairly standard. Before signing any rental contract, make sure the methods of payment are clearly indicated. Finally, remember that your credit card must cover both the rental fees and the deductible in case of an accident. While some credit cards insure you automatically, you should check if the coverage is complete.

A valid driver's license from any country is accepted in the Dominican Republic.

Driving and the Highway Code

In general, the main roads and highways in the Dominican Republic are in good condition, but the odd pothole does crop up here and there.

Table of distances (km)
Via the shortest route

© ULYSSES

									Barahona	
								Higüey	366	
							Jarabacoa	326	248	
						La Romana	244	154	298	
					Monte Cristi	366	270	443	343	
				Puerto Plata	135	309	114	387	421	
			Rio San Juan	83	232	358	147	435	470	
		Samaná	142	226	320	337	212	416	452	
	San Francisco de Macorís	145	119	118	175	230	65	304	339	
Santiago de los Caballeros	55	203	110	60	120	249	50	323	360	
Santo Domingo	157	136	248	270	219	276	89	157	168	204
	San Francisco de Macorís	Santiago de los Caballeros	Samaná	Rio San Juan	Puerto Plata	Monte Cristi	La Romana	Jarabacoa	Higüey	Barahona

Example: the distance beetween Santo Domingo and Puerto Plata is 219 km.

Practical Information

Furthermore, even though there are no shoulders, traffic still moves pretty fast.

Driving on the secondary roads is another story. They are often gravel-covered, narrow and strewn with potholes of all different sizes. Animals also tend to wander across the roads (dogs and chickens, in particular), forcing drivers to brake unexpectedly. Drivers must be particularly careful when passing through villages where there are many pedestrians. Cautious driving is imperative at all times.

Speed bumps have been placed on some village roads to slow down traffic, but unfortunately they are poorly marked. They are usually located on the way into villages and near military barracks.

Road signs, such as speed limit indications, stop signs or no-entry signs are few and far between. The rules of the road are still to be respected, however. Slow down at intersections and do not go over the speed limit of 80 kph. Dominicans drive very fast, often with little regard for these rules, meaning travellers must be particularly vigilant. Many locals do not check their blind spot, and cars equipped with turn signals are rare. Motorcyclists are numerous and quite reckless. Finally, the most hair-raising experiences are almost always associated with passing. There are no passing lanes, except the lane for oncoming traffic. Some drivers weave in and out of traffic, passing at every chance, no matter how slim.

Although significant improvements have been made in recent years, road signs are still insufficient in many places. If you get lost, therefore, the only way of finding your way might be to ask local villagers, who are usually more than happy to help out.

Due to the lack of signs and street lights on Dominican roads, driving at night is strongly discouraged. If your car breaks down you will be stranded. If you do have to drive at night, keep in mind that you are at greater risk of being robbed, so do not pick up hitchhikers or stop at the side of the road, and keep your doors locked.

The speed limit is 80 kph on the highways, 60 kph near cities and 40 kph within city limits.

Accidents

In the event of a road accident, the police will be called to the scene to assess the situation. If there are injuries or damages, witnesses will be asked to testify in court; the information they provide is central to the outcome of the case. Occasionally, the principal witnesses to an accident will be held in jail until the authorities can interview them. The wait can take up to 48hrs. This rarely happens, but should you find yourself in such a situation, stay calm and be patient.

Animals that roam freely along the roads near small villages can be hard to avoid, even for the most careful drivers (chickens seem to be particularly attracted to moving cars). If you do hit one, the local inhabitants might react aggressively, so it is best to drive to the nearest police station and deal with the situation through official channels.

Car Watchers

Throughout the Dominican Republic, youths will offer to wash or keep an eye on your car – for a small fee, of course. Sometimes they will even perform these services without asking, and still expect to get paid. Windshield washers are common at traffic lights. Usually a simple refusal is enough, though sometimes they will wash it anyway. You have every right to refuse to pay; just make sure your windows are up – or you may get a bucket of water in your lap! When it comes to car watchers, it is often best to pay a small sum (to avoid some mysterious scratches appearing on the car). Expect to pay between 10 and 15 pesos for an evening of car surveillance and about 15 pesos for a car wash. Of course, you will have to pay up front.

The Police

Police officers are posted all along Dominican highways. In addition to stopping drivers who break traffic laws, they are authorized to pull over any car they wish and ask to see the identification papers of the driver. The police have been told not to harass tourists, but occasionally some still ask for a few pesos. If you are sure you have not broken any laws, there is no reason to pay anything. Do not be alarmed if the police pull you over to check your papers. In general, they are approachable and ready to help if you have problems on the road.

Gasoline (Petrol)

There are gas stations all over the country. Gas is reasonably priced, generally at par with North American prices. Most stations are open until 10pm, and many stay open 24hrs. More stations are now accepting credit cards.

By Plane

Air Santo Domingo
(☎ 683-8020) connects the main cities of the country.

There are daily flights from Santo Domingo to Puerto Plata, Punta Cana and El Portillo (Samana).

There are daily flights from Punta Cana to Santo Domingo, Puerto Plata, El Portillo (Samana) and La Romana.

There are daily flights from from El Portillo (Samana) to Santo Domingo, Puerto Plata and Punta Cana.

There are daily flights from La Romana to Puerto Plata and Punta Cana.

By Motorcycle or Scooter

In most resort areas, it is possible to rent a motorcycle for $30 to $40 a day. You will need to leave a deposit, such as your passport (or another valid piece of identification) or sometimes even your plane ticket. Drive carefully. Even though motorcycles are common in the Dominican Republic, car drivers are not always cautious around them. Always determine the price and payment conditions before leaving with your rental.

By Taxi

Taxi services are offered in every resort area and medium-sized city. The cars are often very old, but they will get you where you want to go. The rates are fairly high, and are usually posted at the taxi stand. They vary little from one city to another. Make sure to agree on the fare with the driver before starting out, and do not pay until you arrive at your destination.

Puerto Plata

It is possible to get from Puerto Plata to other resort towns by private taxi. In Puerto Plata, there is a taxi stand next to the central park and another in the hotel zone across from Long Beach.

By Motorcyle-Taxi

Motorcyclists offer rides to pedestrians in most cities, providing a quick and inexpensive way to cover short distances. You will have to sacrifice some comfort and security, so avoid long distances and highways. Set a price before getting on; a few kilometres should cost about 10 pesos.

By Collective Taxi (*Públicos*)

In a collective taxi, the cost of the trip is shared between all the passengers, even if their destinations vary. These taxis operate within cities or travel between them. The vehicles are often in terrible shape (especially in Santo Domingo), but are still more comfortable than the bus. They are identifiable by their license plate reading *público*.

By Public Bus (*Guagua*)

Public buses, called *guaguas* by the Dominicans (pronounced "oua-oua"), travel along every type of road in the Dominican Republic and are an efficient way of getting around the island. To catch one, simply go to the local bus station (often near the central park) or wait by the side of a main road and flag one down. These buses stop frequently, and are often jam-packed and very uncomfortable.

On the positive side, this is the cheapest way to get around the island.

Puerto Plata

Guaguas to and from the western part of the island or Santo Domingo stop on Avenida Imbert (the continuation of Avenida Circonvalación Sur), about 500m west of Avenida Colón. For destinations east of Puerto Plata, buses stop in front of the hospital.

Sosúa

Public buses (*guaguas*), heading east or west, stop along the main road. Service is frequent in both directions.

Cabarete

To catch a *guagua* heading east or west, just wait along the main street, which is part of the Atlantic coast highway.

By Coach

Coach service is offered by two bus companies, Metro Bus and Caribe Tours. While these buses are fairly old, they are air conditioned and reasonably comfortable.

Coaches make fewer stops than *guaguas*, and thus cover longer distances quite quickly. The fares are higher than those for *guaguas*, but quicker for long trips.

Puerto Plata

Bus Stops

The following two companies offer inexpensive and direct long-distance bus service aboard air-conditioned vehicles:

Métro
Calle 16 de Agosto corner of Beller
☎ *586-6061*

Caribe Tours
Calle 12 de Julio
☎ *586-4544*

Sosúa

Caribe Tours stops at the edge of Los Charamicos, a few hundred metres from the beach.

Hitchhiking

It is fairly easy to get around the country by hitchhiking. Dominicans are friendly and like chatting with visitors. However, a reasonable amount of caution is advised, especially for women travelling alone.

Financial Services

Currency

The country's currency is the peso. Bills are available in 100, 50, 20, 10, and 5 peso denominations; coins come in 50, 25 and 5 centavo pieces (100 centavos = 1 peso).

Banks

Banks are open Monday to Friday, from 8:30am to 3pm. They can be found in all large and medium-sized cities. Most can exchange US dollars, while fewer deal in other foreign currencies. In certain small villages and on holidays, it is impossible to change money. It is best to carry some cash with you at all times.

Cash advances from your credit card are easy to obtain. Most large banks offer this service. You can also withdraw money using your credit card from automatic teller machines, which are found mostly in Santo Domingo and in a few larger towns.

US Dollars

It is best to travel with cash or traveller's cheques in US dollars since they are easier to exchange and generally fetch a better rate.

Exchanging Money

It is illegal to exchange money on the street. However, in some cities you may be approached by people offering to buy your dollars. It is safer to go to an official currency exchange bureau, especially since the rates are usually about the same.

Traveller's Cheques

It is always best to keep most of your money in traveller's cheques, which are accepted in some restaurants, hotels and shops (if they are in US dollars or pesos). They are also easy to cash at banks and exchange offices. Always keep a copy of the serial numbers of your cheques in a separate place; that way, if the cheques are lost, the company can replace them quickly and easily. Do not rely solely on travellers' cheques. Always carry some cash.

Credit Cards

Most credit cards, especially Visa and MasterCard, are accepted in many businesses. However, many of the smaller places only take cash. Once again, remember that even if you have a credit card and traveller's cheques, you should always have some cash on hand.

When paying with your credit card, always check your receipt carefully to make sure that the abbreviation for the peso – "RDS" – appears, rather than the letters "US". If there is an error, make sure to have it corrected before signing.

Taxes and Service Charges

An 8% tax and a 10% service charge are automatically added to restaurant bills. For hotels, the tax is 5%, and the service charge 6%.

Mail and Telecommunications

Mail

There are post offices in every city, and some hotels offer mailing services and sell stamps. Regardless of where you mail your correspondence from, do not expect it to reach its destination quickly; the postal service in the Dominican Republic is not known for its efficiency. If you have something important to send, you are better off using a fax machine at a Codetel. Stamps are sold in post offices and in some shops.

Telephone and Fax

International telephone calls can be made from the larger hotels or from Codetel centres, which are found in all cities. Calling abroad from a Codetel is very easy. The simplest way is to dial direct, but collect calls can also be made. The length of a call is measured on a computer, and customers pay at a counter when leaving, eliminating the need for handfuls of change. Credit cards are accepted. Codetel centres also offer fax services.

The area code for the entire country is *809*. When calling the Dominican Republic from the United States or Canada, dial *1-809* and the number you wish to reach. Codetel personnel can provide instructions (usually in Spanish, but occasionally in broken English) on how to dial long distance.

Using Foreign Operators

It is possible to use the operator in the country you are calling.

Canada Direct
☎ *1-800-333-0111*

AT&T USA
☎ *1-800-872-2881*

Sprint USA
☎ *1-800-751-7877*
(from pay phone) or *1166* *(wait for tone) 77 (from private phone)*

MCI USA
☎ *1-800-999-9000*

British Telecom Direct
☎ *1-800-751-2701*

Toll-free *1-800* and *1-888* numbers included in this guide can only be reached from North America.

Direct Dialing

Calls dialled directly go through a Dominican operator and are charged accordingly.

To call North America, dial *1*, the area code and the telephone number. For other countries dial *011* then the international country code (see below), the area code and the telephone number.

United Kingdom	**44**
Australia	**61**
New Zealand	**64**
Belgium	**32**
Italy	**39**
Germany	**49**
Netherlands	**31**
Switzerland	**41**

A fruit kiosk where coconuts are sold in abundance.
- *Claude Hervé-Bazin*

Dominican painting depicting everyday life.
- *Dugast*

Fields of sugar cane stretch as far as the eye can see
- *Stéphane G. Marceau*

Tour Guides

You will likely be approached in tourist areas by Dominicans speaking broken English or French, offering their services as tour guides. Some of them are quite capable and trustworthy, but many have little valuable information to share. Be careful. If you want to hire a guide, ask for proof of his or her qualifications. Instead of vending their knowledge at a bargain-basement price, qualified guides will usually charge a substantial fee. Before starting off on a guided tour, establish precisely what services you will be getting and at what price and pay only when the tour is over.

Holidays

All banks and many businesses close on official holidays. Plan ahead by cashing traveller's cheques and doing last-minute souvenir shopping the day before. Things generally slow down during holidays.

January 1
New Year's Day

January 6
Epiphany

January 21
Nuestra Señora de la Altagracia

January 26
Birthday of J.P. Duarte

Variable
Mardi gras

February 27
Independence Day

Variable
Good Friday

May 1
Labour Day

Variable
Corpus Christi

August 16
Restoration of the Republic Day

September 24
Nuestra Señora de las Mercedes

December 25
Christmas Day

Taxes

The Dominican government charges a tax on hotel rooms (see p 111) and another on restaurant bills (see p 131). The tax should be clearly indicated on the bill.

Tips

To show gratitude for good service it is customary to give a tip. In restaurants there is a 10% service charge already added to the total on the bill. In addition to this sum, a tip of 10 to 15% should be left – according to the quality of service, of course.

Electricity

Like in North America, wall sockets take plugs with two flat pins and work on an alternating current of 110 volts (60 cycles). European visitors with electric appliances will therefore need both an adaptor and a converter. There are frequent power cuts in the Dominican Republic. The more expensive hotels compensate with generators.

Women Travelling Alone

Women travelling alone should not encounter any problems in the Dominican Republic. For the most part, people are friendly and not aggressive. Generally, men are respectful toward women, and harassment is uncommon, although Dominican males do have a tendency to flirt. Of course, a certain level of caution should be exercised; avoid making eye contact, ignore any advances or comments and do not walk around alone in poorly-lit areas at night.

Smokers

There are no restrictions with respect to smokers. Cigarettes are not expensive, and smoking is allowed in all public places.

Gay Life

The situation of gays and lesbians in the Dominican Republic is similar to that found in other Latin American countries. Gays still suffer from a certain form of repression, which stems from old family and chauvinistic values and politics. *Machismo*, the notion of male superiority, is alive and well and its insistence upon maintaining rigid, stereotypical gender roles contributes more than anything else to the oppression of homosexuals, while at the same time keeping women in traditional roles.

Prostitution

Veritable scourge of the Dominican Republic, prostitution became rampant in the 1980s following the arrival of masses of tourists. Whether it is male or female prostitution, it exists in the every town that is the least bit touristy. In certain areas, notably Boca Chica and Sosúa, it became such a problem that merchants began to complain. In an effort to restore order, Dominican authorities closed many bars in Sosúa toward the end of 1996.

Time Change

The Dominican Republic is one hour ahead of Eastern Standard Time, and four hours behind Greenwich Mean Time. In the winter it is one hour ahead of New York and Montreal and four hours behind London.

There is no daylight savings time, therefore in the summer it is on the same time as New York and Montreal and five hours behind London.

The Semana Santa

During the days leading up to Easter, called the *Semana Santa* or Holy Week, various festivities are organized by the Catholics to celebrate this auspicious holiday. On Thursday, the pious visit churches throughout the country to pray. On Good Friday the festivities reach their peak as countless processions take to the streets of the country's towns and villages. Many Dominicans take advantage of this holiday to travel within the country, and hotels are often full.

Weights and Measures

Officially, the Dominican Republic uses the metric system. However, businesses often use the imperial system. The following conversions may be helpful.

Weights
1 pound (lb) = 454 grams (g)
1 kilogram (kg) = 2.2 pounds (lbs)

Linear Measure
1 inch = 2.54 centimetres (cm)
1 foot (ft) = 30 centimetres (cm)
1 mile = 1.6 kilometres (km)
1 kilometre (km) = 0.63 miles
1 metre (m) = 39.37 inches

Land Measure
1 acre = 0.4047 hectares (ha)
1 hectare (ha) = 2.471 acres

Volume Measure
1 U.S. gallon (gal) = 3.79 litres
1 U.S. gallon (gal) = 0.83 imperial gallons

Temperature
To convert °F into °C: subtract 32, divide by 9, multiply by 5
To convert °C into °F: multiply by 9, divide by 5, add 32.

Outdoors

Everything has been done to make the Atlantic coast a centre for outdoor activities.

This is one of the main advantages of this region because here you can practise many different aquatic sports, as well as land sports such as golf, horseback riding, bicycling and tennis.

This chapter contains tips and advice on various sports and activities to help you get the most out of them in a safe and environmentally conscious manner.

National Parks

Much of the Dominican Republic's natural beauty is preserved by the island's national parks and its wildlife and science reserves. These wilderness retreats are found in every corner of the country, each protecting a distinct natural environment. There is an increased effort to create infrastructures that would open these areas to visitors, but not all parks are easily accessible. Some, like Parque Los Haïtises near Samaná, and Parque Armando Bermudes around Pico Duarte, are starting to welcome more travellers, and companies have begun organizing excursions there. Others still remain isolated from the resort areas, however, and have virtually no facilities or services to offer. Because some parks are very demanding to explore – containing few, if any, marked trails – the wayfarers who venture in these wild parts should be very careful. Theoretically, to enter a national park, you must have a permit issued by the **National Parks Service** *(Santo Domingo; ☎ 221-5340)*

Permits are also available on site, but often things are poorly organized, and it can be difficult to find the person in charge. The parks, however, are not well supervised. If you are interested in exploring the parks of the Dominican Republic, here is a short description of them.

There are two national parks in the southeastern part of the country:

Located 22km west of Santo Domingo, **Parque Nacional La Caleta** is a marine park that was created to protect the coral reefs and the enormous amount of fish that visit them.

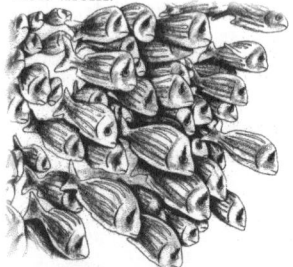

In 1984, a boat was deliberately sunk here to make an artificial reef.

A fascinating park in the southeastern tip of the country, **Parque Nacional del Este** encompasses the small peninsula between Bayahibe and Boca de Yuma, as well as magnificent Isla Saona.

Bordered by sandy beaches and seldom visited, this park has a rich variety of flora and fauna: more than a hundred species of birds, reptiles and marine animals such as the manatee have been sighted here.

There are four national parks in the southwestern part of the country:

Parque Nacional Jaragua is the largest park in the country. It stretches from Perdnales to Oviedo on the tip of the Barahona peninsula. Although the park is difficult to reach, it is definitely worth the visit for its beautiful fine-sand beaches that shelter numerous birds and reptiles.

The small islands of Beata and Alto Velo are also part of the park.

North of the Parque Nacional Jaragua, the **Parque Nacional Sierra de Bahoruco** protects part of the Bahoruco mountain range and is not easily accessible to visitors. The vegetation on the mountain slopes changes with altitude as does the level of precipitation.

The park is known for its **orchids**, of which no less than 166 species have been counted.

Parque Nacional Isla Cabritos is perhaps one of the most fascinating parks in the Dominican Republic. It is located in the middle of Lago Enriquillo, the largest salt-water lake in the Caribbean. This lake attracts unusual fauna, including reptiles and birds such as the pink flamingo. American crocodiles nest on the shores of Isla Cabritos.

The smallest of the parks, **Parque Nacional Laguna Rincón** protects the country's largest freshwater lagoon.

In the country's mountainous centre, there are two national parks and a scientific reserve.

The **Parque Nacional Armando Bermudez** encompasses the northern part of the Cordillera Centrale (766km²) and boasts the Caribbean's highest peak, Pico Duarte, at 3,090m. Tourist facilities are gradually being set up to make the beautiful hike up the mountain less arduous.

Bordering Parque Nacional Armando Bermudez, the **Parque Nacional José del Carmen Ramirez** covers 764km² of the southern Cordillera Central. Like its neighbour, this park has no roads and can only be visited on foot.

The **Reserva Cientifica Valle Nuevo** protects a microclimate with a very special vegetation composed of numerous kinds of trees (mostly conifers) that are normally found in more northerly countries. The temperature can even drop below the freezing mark at certain times of the year.

There are four national parks on the country's northern coast:

Located south of the Samaná Peninsula, the **Parque Nacional Los Haïtises** is relatively easy to explore because there are many organized excursions to it. You can discover amazing mangrove swamp with a diversified wildlife, as well as caves with pre-Colombian drawings.

The **Parque Nacional Isabel de Torres** protects the Pico Isabel de Torres, which is near Puerto Plata. In the past, the summit of this mountain was easily accessible by a cable-car that is now out of service.

The **Banco de la Plata** is a large coral reef north of Puerto Plata. Each year, humpback whales come to these calm waters to reproduce. To protect these marine mammals, the **Parque Nacional Banco de la Plata** was created. The park is difficult to access because of the coral reefs.

Parque Nacional de Monte Cristi covers a large portion of land from Monte Cristi to the Haitian border, including seven small islands, the Cayes Siete Hermanos. The park is frequented by sea turtles, but fewer come each year because they are threatened with extinction from being overhunted.

Outdoor Activities

Swimming

Along the northern coast of the Dominican Republic, there are beaches that are perfect for swimming or just lounging about. The currents can be strong, though, so be careful. You are better off staying close to shore when the waves get high. Also, never swim alone if you don't know how strong the currents are.

Greater efforts have been made to sensitize people about the importance of keeping the beaches clean, especially on the northern coast. Please respect these natural areas.

A completely deserted beach is a rarity in the Dominican Republic. The good beaches are usually overrun with visitors, and to satisfy their every need, vendors roam about selling juice, fruit, beach-wear and souvenirs of all sorts. Generally a "no, gracias" will suffice if you are not interested. Of course, if you look at the merchandise of one vendor, the others will

Outdoor Activities 73

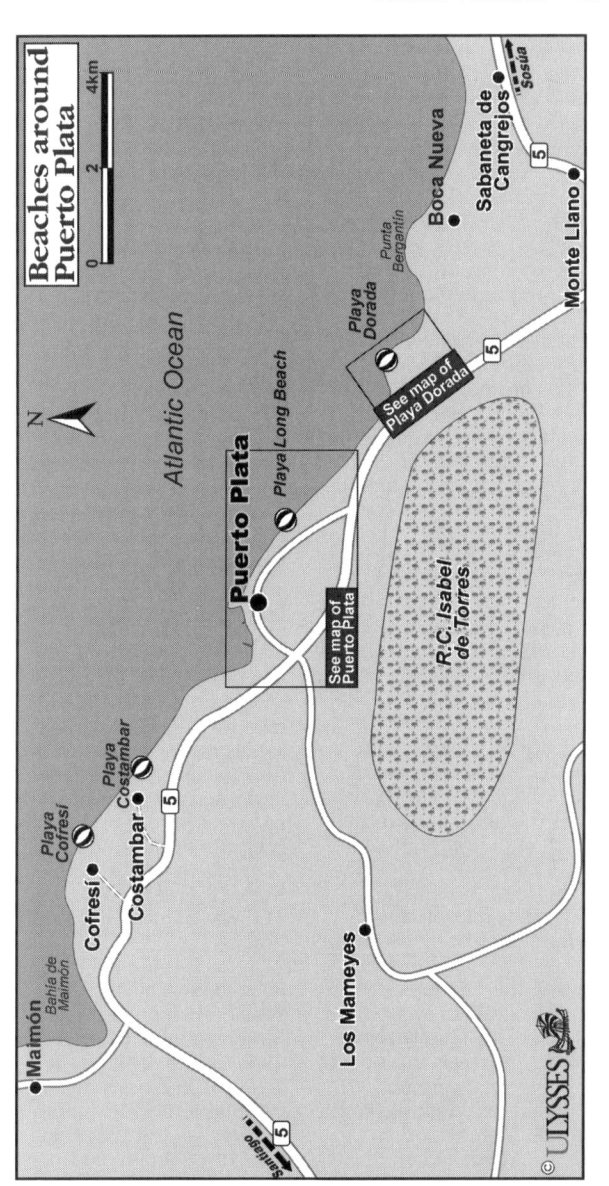

assume you are a potential customer and will come along one by one to hawk their wares. Set a price first if you decide to buy.

Beach chairs and parasols can be rented at almost all beaches near resort towns; the cost is around 20 pesos per day per item.

Beaches are not private in the Dominican Republic. Hotels are nevertheless often built right on the ocean. Anyone can use the beach in front of a hotel, but not necessarily the facilities. These beaches have the advantage of being free of vendors, and are also better maintained.

Here is a short description of some of the long golden-sand crescents along the north shore:

Long Beach extends over several kilometres, lining the seascape of **Puerto Plata**. Unfortunately, this sandy beach is poorly maintained and located much too close to the road to make it a very enjoyable place to swim.

One of the first beaches you'll encounter west of Puerto Plata is **Costambar Beach**, which has the benefit of being relatively uncrowded on week-days. It is a totally different story on the weekends, when city dwellers descend upon the beach in hordes, vying with each other for a piece of this narrow band of sand that will give them access to the rejuvenating effects of the sea.

Surrounded by the large complex of Hacienda Resorts, the **Playa Cofresí ★** is predominately frequented by tourists staying at these hotels. They benefit from a beautiful stretch of fine, white sand, comfortable facilities, and a welcoming stretch of sea.

Playa Dorada ★ consists of a long stretch of blond sand speckled with palm trees, chairs and parasols, thus making it ideal for a pleasant swim. Most of the beach is lined with the large hotels of this popular resort area, so a comfortable terrace for a drink or quick bite is never far away. The beach can get very crowded in winter, when most of the hotel rooms are rented. The prettiest section of the beach is to the west, in front of Jack Tar Village. The waves are also rougher here.

Playa Puerto Chiquito, near Sosúa, presents itself as a long ribbon of white sand divided in half by the Río Sosúa. The bay's waters are calm, and the surrounding scenery is very pretty, as the beach is flanked on both sides by small cliffs. Unfortunately, the waters of the bay are not always that clean and this sometimes detracts from the allure of swimming.

There are two beaches in **Sosúa**: **Playa Sosúa** and **Playa Libre**. Playa Sosúa, a beautiful fine-sand beach about one kilometre long, opens out onto the crystal-clear waters of the bay. The setting is beautiful, but hardly relaxing as the beach is always overrun with tourists and vendors. Restaurants, bars and souvenir stands have been built all along it. It is a noisy place, and the vendors can be very pushy. This is a shame, because the beach is one of the best on the coast. Playa Libre (El Batey neighbourhood) is another option for swimming. This small beach, lined with quality hotels, is quieter and the vendors are less conspicuous here. Less than one kilometre to the east are a few small stretches of sand where you can swim.

A few kilometres before Cabarete, a sign on the left indicates the way to **Playa Punta Goleta**. This splendid beach of delicate sand, rarely frequented and bordered by only a few hotels, will delight aficionados of the more tranquil spots.

Devotees of the longer beaches with a stronger surf are bound to find fulfilment at **Playa Carabete ★★**. Although tourists from the village next door often crowd into the chairs and parasols left at their disposal, it is possible to find a quiet spot in the sand. Carabete spans 3km – perfect for long romantic strolls. The waves can be quite high especially in the afternoon, and windsurfing is very popular here. There are restaurants and terraces close by, and vendors wander about selling their wares.

The seashore of **Río San Juan** includes a few beaches. Those near the Bahía Blanca hotel are pretty and have showers. Small stretches of wild, deserted beach can also be found near the Laguna Gri-Gri. Furthermore, about 2km east of Río San Juan, there is a sign for **Playa Caléton**, which is about a 10-minute walk from the small parking lot by the side of the road. It is also accessible by boat from the Laguna Gri-Gri. This pretty little beach is washed by calm turquoise waters. A few vendors walk about selling food and drinks.

Among the most spectacular beaches in the country, the Playa Grande is remarkable for the sheer length and width of its ribbon of fine sand. Lined with coconut palms from one end to the other for some 2km, **Playa Grande ★★★** is an excellent place to go swimming, despite the occasionally heavy surf. The Caribbean Village hotel complex sits nearby on the western side. Its architects had the good sense not to construct the hotel right on the beach, thereby preserving the harmony of the landscape. There is, however, a small pub on the beach reserved for guests of the Caribbean Village. For those who are not staying at the hotel, vendors rent beach chairs and sell refreshments.

Wild beaches dot the coastline between **Cabrera** and **Nagua**. You can swim here but be careful, the undertow can be very strong and just may carry you out to sea.

Scuba Diving

Playa Dorada, Sosúa, Cabarete and Río San Juan are the main diving centres on the north coast. Many scuba-diving excursions are organized from these centres. Certified divers can explore the secrets of the Dominican coastline to their heart's content. Others can still experience breathing underwater, but must be accompanied by a qualified guide, who will supervise their descent (to a depth of 5m). Although there is little danger, be sure that the supervision is adequate.

Before diving for the first time, it is very important to at least take an introductory course in order to learn basic safety skills: how to clear the water from your mask, how to equalize the pressure in your ears and sinuses, how to breathe underwater (don't hold your breath), to become comfortable with the change in pressure underwater, and to familiarize yourself with the equipment. Many hotels offer a resort course of about one hour before taking first-timers under water. Equipment can easily be rented from the different centres along the coasts.

No matter which diving centre you choose to disembark from, chances are you will be doing it offshore from the Playa Sosúa, which encompasses some of the most intriguing spots. Depending on your level of expertise, you can plunge down into the depths of the water to observe coral reefs, sponge barriers, rock formations, or - better yet - to explore an underwater cave.

Playa Dorada

All of the major hotels organize scuba-diving tours, opening the door to the possibility of exploring the underwater marvels of the Playa Dorada.

Sosúa

Northern Coast Diving
8 Pedro Clisante
☎ *571-1028*
≠ *571-3883*
If the urge to plunge beneath the water is nipping at your heels, Northern Coast Diving is a fine centre from which to disembark. Whether it be your first time diving - or should you wish to obtain your PADI scuba-diving certificate - or perhaps you would like to give night-diving a try - this centre will respond to your wishes. You can count on paying about $55 for an introductory dive, which includes a gear set-up and swimming pool practice, followed by an escorted dive in the afternoon.

Cabarete

Caribbean Divers
Cabarete
☎ *571-0218*
Carabete also runs its own diving centre, Caribbean Divers. The courses offered here cover all kinds of diving, and included among them are some which lead to PADI certification. An introductory dive costs around $55.

Río San Juan

Gri-Gri Divers
☎ *589-2671*
Whether you're a beginner or a seasoned pro, the instructors at Gri-Gri Divers are equipped with the necessary expertise to ensure that your dive is safe and well mapped out. Count on paying roughly $50 for an introductory dive. Expeditions are operated offshore from the Río San Juan.

Snorkelling

It doesn't take much to snorkel: a mask, a snorkel and some flippers. Anyone

Outdoors

can enjoy this activity, which is a great way to develop an appreciation for the richness of the underwater world. Not far from several beaches, you can go snorkelling around coral reefs inhabited by various underwater species. Some companies organize snorkelling trips. Remember that the basic rules for protecting the underwater environment (see scuba diving section) must also be respected when snorkelling.

Sosúa is the most popular place along the coast for this activity. You can rent snorkelling gear or sign up for a sea expedition at one of the following diving centres:

Sosúa

Northern Coast Diving
8 Pedro Clisante
☎ *571-1028*

Cabarete

Caribbean Divers
☎ *571-0218*

Surfing and Windsurfing

If you would like to try these sports, you can rent equipment on the beach, particularly at Cabarete. Some places offer courses, as well.

If you have never tried these sports, a few safety pointers should be followed before hitting the waves: choose a beach where the surf is not too rough; keep well clear of swimmers; don't head too far out (don't hesitate to make a distress signal by waving your arms in the air if you need to) and wear shoes to avoid cutting your feet on the rocks.

Although it is possible to go windsurfing in many places along the coast, **Cabarete** is without a doubt the best spot. Cabarete is not called the "windsurfing capital" for nothing. Its strong winds and protected bay make it one of the top 10 places in the world for this sport. The majority of the hotels along the coast ensure that windsurfing boards are available for their clientele.

Carib Bic Center
☎ *571-0640*
≠ *571-0649*
www.caribwind.com
Windsurfing boards can be rented for $45 for half a day; but there hourly and weekly rates are also available, as are courses.

La Vela
☎ *571-0805*
≠ *571-0856*

Windsurfing boards can also be rented here by the hour (*$20*), the half-day (*$40*), or even the week (*$250*). Courses are also offered to windsurfers of all levels.

Sailing

Excursions aboard sailboats and yachts offer another enchanting way to freely explore the sea's sparkling waves. Some centres organize trips, while others rent sailboats to experienced sailors. You will find a few addresses throughout the guide.

Playa Dorada

Most of the hotel complexes on Playa Dorada offer guests the opportunity to rent small windsurfing boards and catamarans to take them gliding out into the bay.

Dolphins

Excursions, departing from Playa Dorada to Sosua, are organized daily abord a 35-passenger catamaran called the **Freestyle**. These outings last the whole day and include meals and drinks, as well as the prospect of a delightful dip in the ocean or a snorkelling escapade. On certain days, it is even possible to catch a glimpse of a dolphin.

Sosúa

Comfortably settled aboard the **Glass Bottom Boat** (*departures from the beach at 9am and 5pm*), you can explore the depths of the ocean without having to learn the A-B-Cs of deep sea diving. This sea outing, which lasts 45mins, unveils the myriad fish and coral life that live along the Playa Sosúa.

Cabarete

The necessary equipment can be rented on site at two special shops in Cabarete. If the hotel where you are staying does not put windsurfing boards at your disposal, the Carib Bic Center has some for you to take off on the waves, accompanied by an instructor, aboard a catamaran.

Carib Bic Center
$50/hour
☎ **571-0640**

If you prefer, kayaks can be rented from:

Vela
$8/hour
☎ *571-0805*

Deep-Sea Fishing

Deep-sea fishing enthusiasts will be pleased to note that several places offer fishing excursions, particularly out of Playa Dorada and Rio San Juan. Whether you are interested in big fish (like marlin, for example) or smaller ones will determine how far from the island you have to go. These trips usually last about three hours. Equipment and advice are provided. Even if you come back empty-handed, this is still a great way to spend the day.

Deep-sea fishing excursions are not offered in all tourist centres. Sosúa and Playa Dorada are usually the departure points for these outings.

Río San Juan

Two agencies in Río San Juan organize deep-sea fishing expeditions:

Magante Fishing
Calle Duarte
☎ *589-2677*

☎ *589-2600*
around $80.

Campo Tours
☎ *589-2550*
from $70 to $95.

Waterslides

Next to the road between Sosúa and Cabarete, a water park has been built that is guaranteed to please the young and young at heart.

Colombus Aqua Parque
$10 for adults, $6 for children
☎ *571-2642*

Horseback Riding

The Atlantic Coast is an ideal place for excursions on horseback. There is the Cordillera Septentrionale to explore, as well as the coast and countryside. Most of the big hotels offer either half-day or full-day rides.

Río San Juan

It is also possible to embark on an all-day excursion (which includes breakfast) or to simply partake in a one-hour stroll at the:

Rancho de la Esperanza
3-11 Magante
☎ 223-0059

Golf

Golf enthusiasts vacationing on the north coast will be truly spoiled, as there are several excellent courses, several of which are among country's most beautiful.

Playa Cofresí

The Hacienda Golf Course, an 18-hole course bordering the impressive Hacienda Hotel Complex, opened in 1999.

Hacienda Golf Course
☎ *970-7434*

Playa Dorada

Playa Dorada's 18-hole golf course, designed by Robert Trent Jones, has what it takes to lure even the most discriminating of golfers. Extending out over part of the beach, it is situated at a prime spot close to the major hotels, some lush gardens, and, of course, the ocean.

Playa Dorada
☎ *320-3803*

Playa Grande

While the greens at Playa Dorada have earned the acclaim of countless golf enthusiasts, a new 18-hole course on Playa Grande is posing a serious challenge to its ranking as the golfing mecca of the North Coast. Nothing has been overlooked in the design of the striking 18-hole grounds of the Playa Grande. Located on the summit of some steep cliffs overlooking the ocean, the site is nothing short of exceptional, providing golfers with the double advantage of a challenging golf course and an alluring panorama of the coast.

Playa Grande
☎ *248-5313*

Birdwatching

Numerous species of birds can be seen along the Atlantic coast, be it on the beaches, in the forests or in the countryside: cattle egrets, hummingbirds, turtledoves and especially pelicans.

Rio San Juan

One spot guaranteed to have some winged activity

is the **Laguna Gri-Gri**, at the Río San Juan, the nesting grounds of many species, most notably the hummingbird.

Most can be observed during a boat tour of the lagoon, or during a walk to the lagoon (*easy access from the end of the Bahía Blanca Hotel road*).

Exploring

Some people go to the north coast of the Dominican Republic for its magnificent white-sand beaches, some of which are among the most beautiful in the Caribbean.

Resorts have been built on these beaches for every taste and budget; others prefer the splendid mountain scenery and lush vegetation of the Cordillera Septentrionale. Whatever the reason, this region has plenty to please all types of travellers.

Some people will also want to visit other regions of the country, so one-day excursions are organized from the main towns on the north coast. These excursions go to some of the most fascinating towns in the Dominican Republic, such as Santo Domingo, the 500-year-old capital city that has preserved treasures from its colonial past, and Jarabacoa, a charming little town up in the mountains in the middle of the country. Both cities reveal a different face of the Dominican Republic.

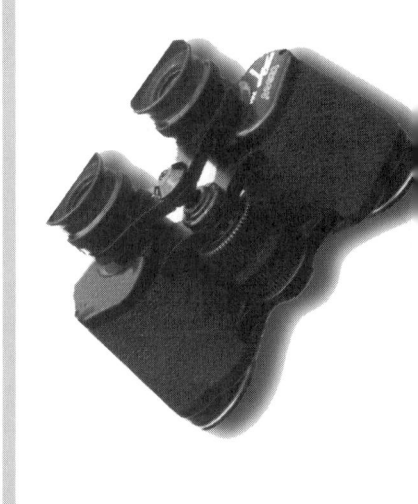

★★ Puerto Plata

Puerto Plata was founded in the early days of Spanish colonization (1502) by Nicolás de Ovando, in order to give the Spanish fleet a port on the northern coast of the island. Its first years were prosperous, but with the discovery of riches elsewhere in the Americas, the port of Puerto Plata became less important to the Spanish Crown.

To make up for the lack of activity in their city, the residents of Puerto Plata began dealing in contraband with the French and English. To reaffirm its power and put a stop to smuggling in the area, the Crown ordered that the city of Puerto Plata be destroyed and abandoned a century after it was founded.

The city was not rebuilt until 1742, when a few Spanish families arrived from the Canary Islands. Once again, the city became an important seaport used for shipping out natural resources and agricultural products from the centre of the country. Today Puerto Plata is a lively, medium-sized urban centre with the busiest seaport on the northern coast.

The city's beautiful location, nestled between the Atlantic Ocean and the Cordillera Septentrionale mountain range, adds to its allure. Despite the constant development in Puerto Plata, its downtown has remained largely unchanged, retaining its typical Caribbean flavour. A number of Victorian and Republican buildings from the last century still line the avenues near the **Parque Duarte**, where most of the commercial activity takes place.

The main tourist facilities in Puerto Plata are located on the east side of the city, near **Long Beach** and its pleasant promenade. Since Long Beach is not very good for swimming, many visitors head for the beaches just outside Puerto Plata.

The **Fortaleza San Felipe de Puerto Plata** ★ (*$1; at the western end of the malecón*) is located on a point of land that juts into the ocean at the western edge of the city. Built in the 16th century to defend the port against pirates, this massive fortress is the only remnant of Puerto Plata's first period of colonization. At several points in its history the fort served not only to defend the city but also as a penitentiary.

Exploring 85

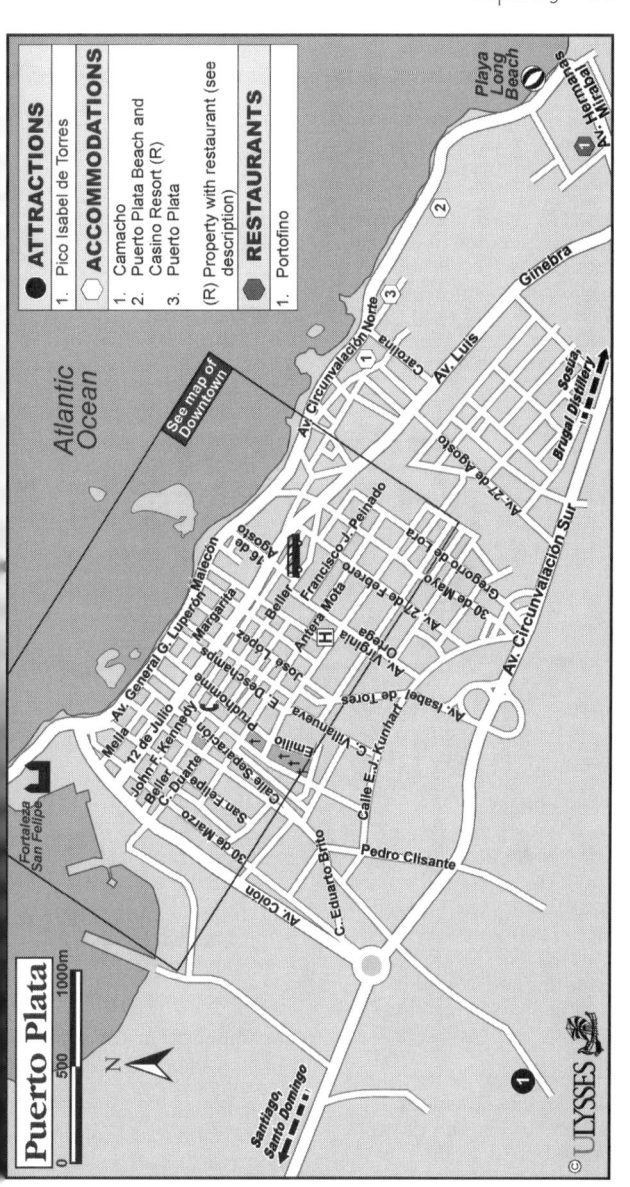

Visitors will find a small military museum, as well as the cell that held the great hero of the country's war of independence, Juan Pablo Duarte, in 1844.

The site has a good view of the city, the ocean and the mountains. To get there, walk to the end of the **malecón ★**, the long promenade that runs alongside the ocean for several kilometres.

the lively neighbouring streets you will find restaurants, market stalls and stores, while the park itself is surrounded by Victorian buildings.

The beautiful **Glorieta ★**, whose construction dates back to 1872, stands at the centre of the park. The **Iglesia San Felipe**, an Art Deco church with a very sober interior, dating from 1934, also stands on the south side of the park.

Glorieta

In the evening, the malecón is a popular meeting place for Dominican families and couples, and countless stalls selling snacks and drinks line the sidewalks.

Parque Central ★ (*at the corner of Calles Beller and Separacíon*) is one of the busiest areas in the city. On

Also minutes from the park is the **Museum of Taino Art** (*Calle San Felipe, corner of Beller*).

The **Museo del Ámbar ★★** (*$2.50; Mon to Sat 9am to 6pm; at the corner of Calles Prudhomme and Duarte,* ☎ *586-2848*) located in a neoclassical building that

Exploring 87

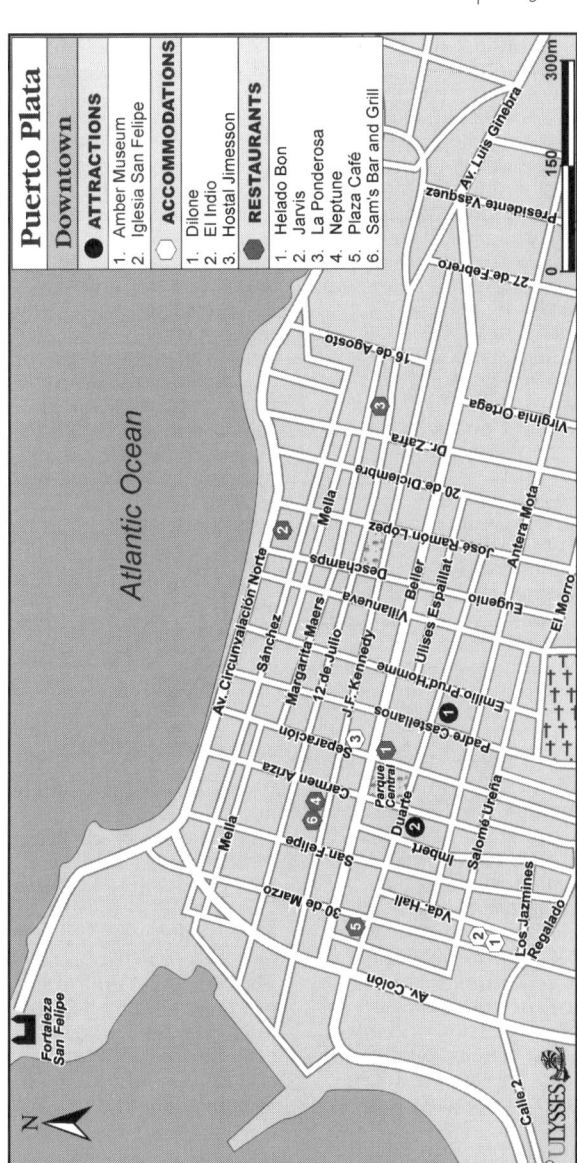

Puerto Plata
Downtown

ATTRACTIONS
1. Amber Museum
2. Iglesia San Felipe

ACCOMMODATIONS
1. Dilone
2. El Indio
3. Hostal Jimesson

RESTAURANTS
1. Helado Bon
2. Jarvis
3. La Ponderosa
4. Neptune
5. Plaza Café
6. Sam's Bar and Grill

was built in 1918, has a small but beautiful collection of amber, the fossilized resin found throughout the Dominican Republic. A succession of little display windows protect some interesting specimens, several containing insects – especially beetles – as well as some plants trapped in amber during the early stages of its genesis. You can further enhance your knowledge and appreciation of amber by hiring a guide, or by taking a few moments to read the informative panels that trace the origins and the creation of this fascinating resin. The little shop below the museum has a good selection of souvenirs, including jewellery made of amber and larimar, a pretty blue stone also found in the Dominican Republic.

One of the most popular attractions in town for a long time now, the **cable car** up to the summit of **Pico Isabel de Torres** ★★ *($2; about 500m out of town to the west, a well-marked 500m trail leads to the cable car)* was unfortunately undergoing renovations at press time. Be sure to check on the progression of the work before heading all the way there. Though some taxi drivers are willing to take you all the way up to the summit, be aware that the road leading you there is very steep and dangerous. From its highest point, at 793m above sea-level, the Pico Isabel de Torres provides an exceptional view of Puerto Plata and the surrounding beaches, mountains and towns. At the summit there is an impressive statue of Christ the Redeemer and trails leading through the flowering gardens. This mountain is in the centre of the **Reserva Científica Isabel de Torres**. Vegetation such as wild tamarinds and Hispaniola mahoganies grow in the reserve and some 32 kinds of birds can be observed.

Green Heron

If you are curious to know how rum is made, tours are offered at the **Brugal Rum Distillery** *(free guided tours; Mon to Fri 9am to noon and 2pm to 4pm; 500m outside of town heading east, buildings are visible from the road)*. This small modern distillery produces about 1,300,000 litres of white and dark rum each year, 95% of which is consumed in the Dominican Republic. The tour of the premises is short, amounting to little more than a look at the bottling process. However, the guides can provide a wealth of information on the rum industry. There is also a small kiosk that sells souvenirs sporting the Brugal logo, as well as the different varieties of the famous rum at a slight discount.

Baseball fans will be happy to learn that it is almost certain that the next baseball team in the Dominican Republic professional league will be in Puerto Plata.

October to January is baseball season in the Dominican Republic. Games are played at **Quisqueya Stadium** (☎ 565-5565). Games start at 7:30pm on weekdays and 4pm on weekends. Tickets go for anywhere between $1 and $10, and fans will not be disappointed because Dominican baseball is professional – even some American players come to practise with Dominican teams off-season, during the winter months. Many Dominicans have also made it to the Major Leagues.

Humpback whales also come to the calm waters of the Atlantic Ocean north of Puerto Plata where they are protected by a coral reef. A number of these whales reproduce here. The 3,700-km² **Banco de la Plata Reserve** was created to protect this area. Because navigating on the coral reefs is dangerous, virtually no whale-watching excursions are offered.

Costambar

Costambar is located three kilometres west of Puerto Plata. From there (there is a sign), a dirt road leads to Costambar after 1km.

Costambar lies alongside the first small **beach** west of Puerto Plata. It is a peaceful, fairly undeveloped area with few hotels, but a fair number of villas belonging to foreigners or wealthy Dominicans. A nine-hole golf course is located nearby, while a few restaurants, a motorcycle rental shop and some markets round out the facilities on site. Few vacationers end up staying here, most come for the golf course or the beach.

Playa Cofresí

Still on the main highway, but a few kilometres west of Costambar, a well-marked road branches off and leads directly to Playa Cofresí after about 1km.

Recent years have seen considerable growth in Playa Cofresí, due mainly to the opening of the large **Hacienda Resorts** complex, which includes several hotels. The site also includes many private villas, fine restaurants, grocery stores and various other businesses. The main reason for coming here, the pretty little white-sand **beach ★**, remains unchanged.

Playa Dorada

From Costambar or Playa Cofresí, you will have to retrace your steps and go through Puerto Plata to reach Playa Dorada. It is about three kilometres east of Puerto Plata on the main road.

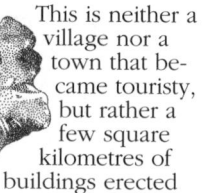

This is neither a village nor a town that became touristy, but rather a few square kilometres of buildings erected solely for tourism. It has about a dozen luxury hotels offering a wide range of services and activities.

The area is very pleasantly landscaped with lovely gardens, hibiscus bushes, a few ponds, a superb 18-hole golf course designed by Robert Trent Jones and a beautiful long white-sand **beach ★**. Visitors can enjoy a wide range of water sports, set off on excursions and adventures into the surrounding region or simply relax with a drink on one of the many terraces. For many years now, Playa Dorada has been the most popular of the large resort areas. It is perfect for travellers looking for a beautiful, safe seaside resort with luxury hotels and all the modern comforts. Those in search of more of an introduction to the Dominican culture and way of life, however, will be somewhat disappointed. Playa Dorada is accessible from Highway 5, which follows the northern coast.

Puerto Chiquito

Continue along Highway 5 for about 20km. About 1.5km before Sosúa, a large colourful sign clearly marks the road to Puerto Chiquito. The village lies less than a kilometre away.

Located a bit more than one kilometre west of Sosúa, Puerto Chiquito lies alongside a pretty little bay surrounded by towering rocky cliffs. The setting is definitely worth a look, especially from the terrace of the Sand Castle hotel, which offers a stunning panoramic view of the ocean. The white-sand **beach**, divided in two by the Río

Sosúa, is several hundred metres long. It is used mostly by guests of the Sand Castle, who enjoy all manner of water sports in the calm waters of the bay. The water here is unfortunately not very clean.

★★

Sosúa

The city of Sosúa consists of the Los Charamicos and El Batey neighbourhoods. These two areas are separated by a long, sandy beach. When coming from Puerto Plata, you will pass by Los Charamicos first, then El Batey, about 1km farther along, where most of the hotels are located.

Sosúa was little more than a small banana-growing centre when a group of European Jews took refuge here in the 1940s. The president at the time, the dictator Trujillo, agreed to welcome these refugees in an effort to improve his poor international reputation. The new arrivals were to have a significant impact on the development of Sosúa, especially its economy, by setting up the prosperous dairy and livestock farms for which the region is known. A number of these refugees and their descendants still live in the area. The city they helped build seems to have escaped them, however, lost to the ever-increasing throngs of tourists. Their synagogue, for example, looks out of place among the restaurants, bars, nightclubs and hotels, as if it belonged to another era and another civilization.

In fact, with the exception of Puerto Plata, Sosúa has undergone more tourist development than any other area on the coast, and the general appearance of the city has unfortunately suffered as a result. Little remains of its traditional architecture, and large parts of the city are devoted completely to commerce. The ambience has also changed considerably; vendors of all sorts have become pushier, and prostitution is flourishing (the government intervened in 1996 in an attempt to ban prostitution and return a certain respectability to the city).

Nevertheless, Sosúa can still be a pleasant place to stay, due to its abundance of restaurants, hotels and outdoor diversions. The jagged coastline makes for some beautiful landscapes, and the bay's waters are always crystal-clear.

Sosúa has two beaches: **Playa Sosúa ★**, about one kilometre long and always

Exploring

crowded, and **Playa Libre**, smaller but also much calmer.

The two neighbourhoods located on either side of the bay are separated by Playa Sosúa. Most of the hotels and tourist development is on the east side, in the **El Batey** neighbourhood, which is also home to several beautiful residences. The **Los Charamicos** neighbourhood has remained essentially residential, thus preserving a typical small-town Dominican atmosphere.

Sosúa's **Sinagoga** (*Calle Alejo Martinez*) is a small, modest-looking building still used as a place of worship by the city's Jewish community.

Right next door is the **Museo de Sosúa** (*free admission; 6pm to 11pm; Alejo Martinez*), whose mission is to inform visitors about the city's history. Historical documents and personal objects belonging to Sosúa's first Jewish settlers are on display.

From the outskirts of Sosúa, visitors can enjoy beautiful excursions to the Cordillera Septentrionale on the Carretera Turistica. This highway is closed to big trucks and offers magnificent **views** ★ of the mountainous landscape of the Cordillera all the way to Santiago de los Caballeros in the centre of the country. The Carretera Turistica starts along the main road midway between Sosúa and Puerto Plata. The drive to Santiago takes about an hour.

Punta Goleta

To reach Punta Goleta from Sosúa, follow the highway for about 10km.

The pretty, sandy **beach** of Punta Goleta runs along the ocean for a few hundred metres and is an extension of the superb Playa Cabarete. The beach is not particularly crowded, as there are few big hotels nearby. Pretty thatched parasols have been set up on the sand for shade.

★★

Cabarete

Continue east on the highway to Cabarete.

Cabarete is considered the windsurfing capital of the country, and with good reason. The conditions for this sport are excellent, especially on windy summer days. Cabarete has actually become somewhat famous; each June windsurfing professionals gather here to take part in an international competition. Windsurfing is not the only reason to go to Cabarete, however. Its magnificent **beach** ★★ stretches nearly three kilometres, making it perfect for long walks. Contrary to the beach at Sosúa, for example, Cabarete's beach is large enough that you don't feel hemmed in on all sides by hotels and sunbathers.

Though tourism has become the mainstay of the village's economy, Cabarete has retained a pleasant, casual atmosphere and also offers a good selection of hotels, generally small or medium-sized, as well as several restaurants. Those who choose to stay here will also find themselves well situated for excursions along the Atlantic coast.

Behind the village, there is an interesting **lagoon**, where the comings and goings of several species of birds, including pelicans, can be observed.

To visit Cabarete's **caves** ★ (*$12; take the road near the Codetel, on the west side of Cabarete, for 1 km to the Cabarete Adventure Park*), you must be accompanied by a guide from the Cabarete Adventure Park, the only outfit with the rights to market this place. The three-hour guided tour leads through the countryside and a tropical forest, but unfortunately includes several uninteresting stops along the way. Once at the caves, however, you are allowed to look around and swim in one of the natural pools. The caves are interesting, but the rest of the tour is uninspiring, and the guides and owner of the place are downright unpleasant.

Gaspar Hernández

An unremarkable but always busy little coastal town, Gaspar Hernández is a little more than 15km from Cabarete on the road to Río San Juan and Samaná. The town has a few banks and gas stations, a Codetel, and some small, inexpensive hotels of dubious quality.

Playa Magante

About halfway between Gaspar Hernandez and Río San Juan, a sign on the highway indicates the direction of Playa Magante. Along this small, sandy beach, which is a great place to swim, you will find some good restaurants.

★
Río San Juan

Río San Juan is about 30km east of Gaspar Hernández. To reach the beach of the Bahía Blanca hotel, follow the lagoon shore to the left

Río San Juan is a pleasant fishing village in an area known for farming and dairy production, where life still revolves around the sea. Some of the village streets, with their small houses painted in pastel shades, correspond to the romantic images people often have of small Caribbean towns.

Although most visitors come here to visit the famous Laguna Gri-Gri and its striking stands of tangled, tropical mangrove trees, Río San Juan has enough to offer to make a longer stay worthwhile. The region is full of enchanting landscapes, and beautiful sandy **beaches** line the shore in front of the friendly little Bahía Blanca hotel. There are several other small beaches, virtually deserted most of the time, around the lagoon. And finally, about two kilometres west of Río San Juan, is **Playa Caletón**, accessible either by boat from the Laguna Gri-Gri, or by foot from the road towards Cabrera.

Laguna Gri-Gri is accessible from the highway by following Calle Duarte, the main road in Río San Juan.

Boats are always available for visits to the **Laguna Gri-Gri ★★** (*$26 per boatload of up to 15 people; departure from the end of Calle Duarte, at the corner of Calle Sanchez*).

The tour leads around the lagoon all the way to the ocean, through a magnificent mangrove forest where a variety of tropical bird species can be observed at close range. The excursion continues along the coastline to a small inlet called La Piscina, whose crystalline waters are perfect for swimming. You will also stop at Playa Caleton long enough for another swim before returning to the lagoon. Those who would like to spend more time bird-watching around the lagoon can get there on foot by following the main road of the Bahía Blanca hotel to the end. Early morning is the best time to observe and photograph birds.

El Barrio Acapulco (*near the ocean on the west side of town*) is a working-class neighbourhood where most of the fishermen in Río San Juan live. Those interested in boat-building and fishing will appreciate a visit to this unfortunately very poor area.

★★★

Playa Grande

About eight kilometres from Río San Juan is Playa Grande, without a doubt one of the most impressive beaches in the country. This long crescent of white sand extends for some two kilometres between a splendid bay and a string of palm trees. The surrounding scenery is lovely, and the hardy waves delight swimmers and surfers alike. The large Caribbean Village Hotel Complex opened near the beach in 1994; fortunately, it has not marred the beautiful setting. Most beach-goers here are either guests at this hotel, or part of organized tours from Playa Dorada, Sosúa, Cabarete or elsewhere. Nevertheless, Playa Grande is still the least crowded beach of this calibre in the western part of the country.

Cabrera

A few kilometres further along, the highway passes along the outskirts of Cabrera. To reach Cabrera from the highway, follow the small road on the left side. Watch carefully because it is poorly marked and located in a curve in the road.

Cabrera is a typical Dominican coastal town pleasantly located on a small cape. While it has no major attractions, the view of the ocean and the cliffs nearby is spectacular. A good spot to take in this beautiful seaside panorama is at the **Parque Nacional Cabo Frances Viejo** *(2 km before Cabrera)*, a small protected area along the coast. It is a quiet, virtually deserted spot, where you can observe the waves crashing into the surrounding cliffs. This is a good place for a picnic. There are a number of interesting undeveloped beaches close by, but most are hard to get to. You will need a good map and directions from the locals to find them.

A visit to the brand new **Amazone 2** *($3; east of Cabrera)* ecological park offers a chance to take an interesting 20min walk in a dense forest, where you can see some of the plants typical of this region and learn about certain aspects of the local geology. Before setting out, you will be given a small map indicating the various points of interest in the park (marsh plant zone, fern valley, bat cave, etc.). Visitors will also find a gigantic canvas aviary containing a variety of birds, and another, smaller one sheltering scores of pretty butterflies.

★ The Palm Tree Route

For over 10km, the road between Cabrera and Nagua runs alongside the ocean through a striking palm grove. After cutting across the palm grove to the shore, you will find some superb wild beaches. If you decide to swim, be very careful because the current and undertow can be very strong here.

Nagua

Highway 5 passes through the town of Nagua. The road forks here, with one side (to the left) heading to the Samaná Peninsula, and the other (to the right) to San Francisco de Macorís.

Nagua is a medium-sized town at the intersection of the roads from Puerto Plata and San Francisco de Macorís, and anyone on their way to the magnificent Samaná Peninsula must inevitably pass through here. It has a number of commercial streets, gas stations, and a **Parque Central** (*Calle Duarte*), where several restaurants can be found. As the town is of little interest, few visitors passing through it decide to stay. There are, however, a few lovely, undeveloped beaches farther south, between Nagua and the Samaná Peninsula, with a few small hotels nearby.

Excursion to Santo Domingo

The first city founded in the Americas, Santo Domingo has some 500 years of history under its belt.

In 1496, after a fruitless effort to colonize the north shore of the island, Bartolomé, son of the great Genoese admiral Christopher Columbus, decided to build a city on the shores of the Caribbean Sea, at the mouth of the Río Ozama. Founded on the east bank of the river, this city was christened Nueva Isabel.

A colourful bus at a bustling Dominican market.
- *Claude Hervé-Bazin*

Playa Cabarete, one of the most popular beaches in the country
- *T. Philiptcher*

The Laguna Gri-Gri is an exceptional site where a multitude of bird species can be observed.
- *Claude Hervé-Bazin*

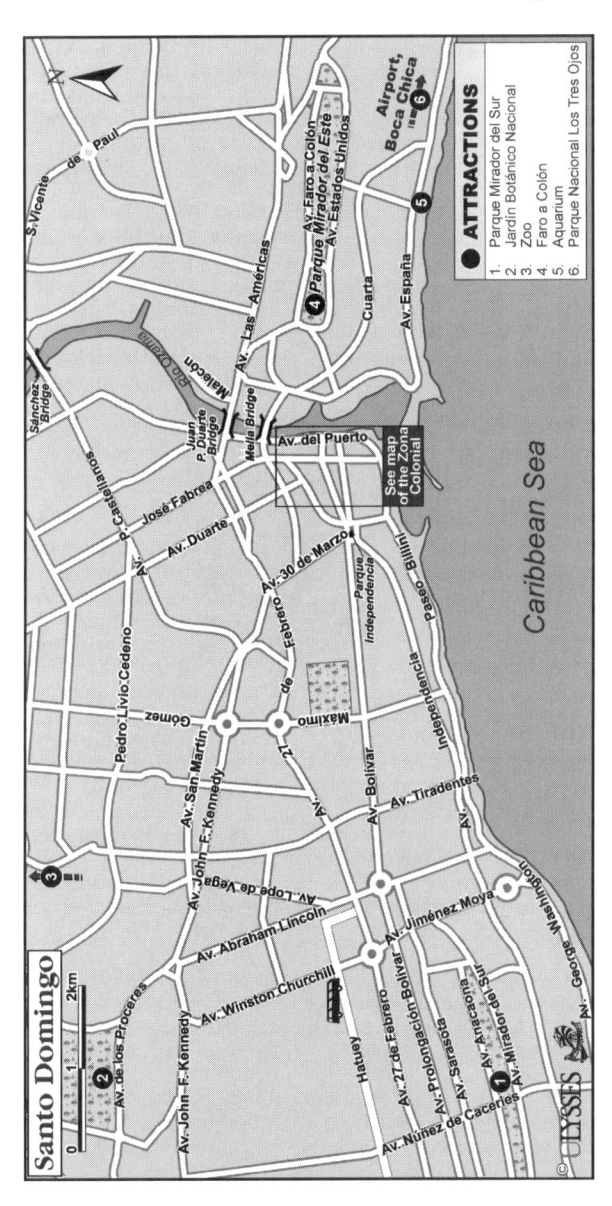

Excursion to Santo Domingo 97

ATTRACTIONS
1. Parque Mirador del Sur
2. Jardín Botánico Nacional
3. Zoo
4. Faro a Colón
5. Aquarium
6. Parque Nacional Los Tres Ojos

Exploring

A hurricane destroyed its first buildings, however, and in 1502, Nicolás de Ovando, the colonial governor at the time, decided to reconstruct the town on the west bank of the Ozama, a location he deemed more strategic.

The seat of the government of Spain's colonies in the New World, Santo Domingo thrived right from the start, and the numerous buildings dating from that period serve as evidence of this. Spain began losing interest in Santo Domingo in 1515, when the island's gold mines were finally exhausted and fabulous riches were discovered elsewhere, most notably in Peru and Mexico, prompting the authorities to relocate the colonial government. Despite its decline in relation to the other Spanish colonies, Santo Domingo remained a nerve centre and continued to play a major role in the development of the country.

It was not long before Europe's other great powers began to show interest in the New World colonies, and, envying the riches Spain had found there, tried to conquer them. Wars, invasions and destruction thus became the lot of the colonists. Santo Domingo was no exception, and many of its buildings were destroyed in an attack by English pirate Sir Francis Drake in 1586. An English offensive in 1655 and French domination from 1795 to 1809 disrupted life in the capital, whose inhabitants managed, often through bitter combat, to resist and drive back the invaders. In the mid-19th century, Haitian troops invaded the country and took control of it in 1822.

The 19th century brought a desire for independence, which changed the course of Dominican history. Juan Pablo Duarte, a fervent defender of these aspirations, succeeded in gaining the country's independence from Haiti in 1844. Santo Domingo was named capital of the Dominican Republic. The young republic was not safe from invaders, however, and was repeatedly attacked by Haitian troops, which the Dominicans, with considerable difficulty, succeeded in driving back. Less than 20 years later, in 1861, Spain annexed the country once again, putting an end to its independence and stripping Santo Domingo of its status as capital. This annexation only lasted a short time, however, and in 1865, the country was declared independent once and for all. Santo Domingo has been the capital ever since. Only its name has changed; during the Trujillo (1930-1961) dictatorship, the generalissimo renamed it Ciudad Trujillo (1936). Immediately following the president's death, the city became Santo Domingo again.

Trujillo's death also had harsh consequences for the capital, however, as it sparked major social unrest. The climate was so unstable that the Americans deemed it necessary to intervene to put some order back into the country's internal affairs. In 1965, American troops entered Santo Domingo and shelled parts of the old city, damaging a number of old buildings.

Today, with over 2,000,000 inhabitants, Santo Domingo is the largest and most populated city in the Dominican Republic. It is the country's financial, industrial and commercial centre. Its petrochemical, metallurgical, textile and plastic industries are thriving. It also has the busiest port in the country. Despite the frantic pace of life here, Santo Domingo is a pleasant city, especially in the colonial zone. Nicolás Ovando drew up the plans for the city in 1502. With the aim of reducing the existing traffic problems, he used a grid pattern for the streets. Elsewhere, however, the city has not always developed in such an organized manner.

★★

The Zona Colonial

To visit the Zona Colonial is to climb streets that are imbued with memory and history, discovering buildings that may be as much as 500 years old, to marvel at the still palpable colonial past. For those interested in old stonework, this is doubtless the most rewarding visit in the country. A stroll through these streets is even more pleasant than it is effortless, the buildings being set in a relatively limited perimeter and the traffic being much lighter than in nearby downtown.

Once called "Mayor Place", **Parque Colón** *(at the corner of Calle Arzobispo Meriño an Calle El Conde)*, at the center of which stands a bronze stature of the Genoese sailor, is the departure point for the tour. Many guided tours leave from this park and buses full of tourists stop here in great numbers, which explains the hordes of vendors and self-proclaimed private-tour guides who make the park less pleasant than one would hope.

The magnificent **Catedral Santa María de la Encarnacíon** ★★★ (*facing Parque Colón*), constructed during the 1540s on the order of Real Miguel de Pasamonte, dominates an entire side of the park. It is famous as the first cathedral constructed in the Americas and also constitutes the oldest building of the Plateresque-Gothic style (which allies the characteristics of Gothic and Spanish Renaissance architectural styles with baroque ornamentation).

From the outside, this squat grey-stone building may seem dull, but it conceals an extremely beautiful interior. First, there is its elegant door and then, once your eyes have adjusted to the dimly-lit interior, its graceful arches, its magnificent mahogany altar dating from 1684 and its 14 little chapels dispersed on either side of the cathedral. Until 1992 one of these chapel enclosed the tomb of Christopher Columbus, which is now located at the Faro a Colón. After being left to deteriorate over many years, the cathedral has recently been restored. Visits to the cathedral are free. Proper dress (no shorts or mini-skirts) is required.

The **Palacio de Borgella** (*on Isabel la Católica, facing Parque Colón*), dates from the 19th century, and was once the seat of executive power for the country. It now houses administrative offices.

The **Casa Diego Caballero** and The **Casa Sacramento** (*Calle Pellereno Algaz*) both face a small cobblestone lane, the first pedestrian street in Santo Domingo. The latter was home to many important colonial figures, including archbishop Alonso de Fuenmayor, who ordered the construction of the city walls. The Casa Diego Caballero was built around 1523. Its façade is distinguished by two square towers, while its interior features galleries formed by solid stone arches.

Keep walking until you reach Calle Las Damas.

Calle Las Damas ★★★

Calle Las Damas is like nothing else in Santo Domingo. This splendid little street, where some of the oldest and most beautiful buildings in the old city stand in succession, will doubtless be inscribed in your memory and constitute one of the most remarkable moments of your trip.

Excursion to Santo Domingo 101

Santo Domingo
Zona Colonial

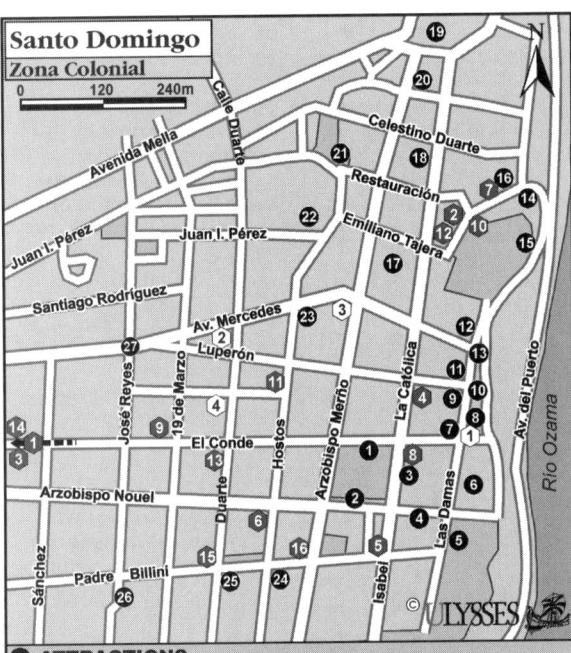

0 120 240m

● ATTRACTIONS

1. Parque Colón
2. Cathedral Santa María de la Encarnación
3. Palacio de Borgellá
4. Casa de Diego Caballero and the Casa Del Sacramento
5. Fortaleza de Santo Domingo
6. Casa de Batisdas
7. Casa de Hernán Cortés
8. Casa de Nicolás de Ovando
9. Panteón Nacional
10. Capilla de Los Remedios
11. Casa des Jésuites
12. Museo de Las Casas Reales
13. Reloj de Sol
14. Alcázar de Colón
15. Fuerte San Diego
16. Calle Atarazana
17. Casa del Cordón
18. Museo de Juan Pablo Duarte
19. Fuerte y Iglesia Santa Bárbara
20. Museo de Ambar
21. Ermita de San Antón
22. Monasterio de San Francisco
23. Hospital San Nicolás
24. Imperial Convento de Santo Domingo
25. Capilla de la Tercera Orden de Los Dominicos
26. Iglesia Regina Angelorum
27. Iglesia Conventual de las Mercedes

○ ACCOMMODATIONS

1. Hostal Nicolás de Ovando
2. Hostal Nader
3. Hotel Frances
4. Hotel Palacio

● RESTAURANTS

1. Bariloche
2. Brasserie Pat'e Palo
3. Café de Las Flores
4. Café Galería
5. Coco's Restaurant
6. De Nosotros
7. Fonda Atarazana
8. L'Avocat
9. La Cafetería
10. La Crêperie
11. Meson D'Bari
12. Museo del Jamón
13. Panadería Sum
14. Petrus Cafetería
15. Retazos
16. Ristorante La Briciola

Exploring

Fortaleza Santo Domingo ★ (*10 pesos; Mon to Sat 9am to 5pm, Sun 10am to 3pm; Calle Las Damas*), the oldest military building in the Americas, stands proudly at the edge of a cliff presiding over both the Caribbean and Río Ozama, a location originally chosen for its strategic value in the protection of the colony.

Fortaleza Santo Domingo

The walls surrounding this vast military complex shelter an attractive garden, at the center of which stands a statue of Gonzales de Oviedo, which you will notice upon entering. The munitions building is located to the right of the entrance. At the end of the garden, there is a square structure known as the **Torre del Homenaje**, whose construction began in 1505 by order of Nicolás de Ovando.

The **Casa de Bastidas** (*Calle Las Damas*) was built at the beginning of the 16th century for Don Rodrigo de Bastidas, a comrade of Nicolás de Ovando, who arrived in Santo Domingo in 1502. The neoclassical portal was added in the 17th century. A charming inner garden enhances the beauty of the residence. Two small art galleries have been set up in the rooms adjoining the entrance.

The **Casa de Hernán Cortes** (*Calle Las Damas*) was constructed in the early 16th century to accommodate representatives of public institutions. It has been restored and now houses the offices of the Maison de la France (French Tourist Board). It was from here that Cortés planned the conquest of Mexico.

Now a hotel, the **Hostal Palacio Nicolás de Ovando** (*Calle Las Damas*) was the residence of the governor of the colony from 1502 to 1509. Nicolás de Ovando was an important figure in Santo Domingo's history, as he enhanced the city's development by instituting various construction standards. The house is certainly among the most beautiful and elegant residences of its era. Built of high quality cut stones, it has a Gothic-style portal, a very rare feature in the architecture of the New World.

Once a Jesuit church, the **Panteon Nacional** ★ (*every day 9am to 4:40pm; Calle Las Damas*) was built between 1714 and 1745. This imposing neoclassical church is made of large grey stones; a sculpted Dominican coat of arms adorns the façade. The interior consists of a single nave hung with magnificent wrought-iron chandeliers. In 1950, Trujillo ordered that the building be renovated and transformed into a pantheon in honour of the country's heroes. Although it is open to the public, dress appropriately (no shorts or mini skirts) to visit it.

During the 16th century, the **Capilla de Nuestra Señora de los Remedios** (*Calle Las Damas*) was a private church belonging to a wealthy family, the Davilas. The pretty little red brick chapel has a campanile with three arches. The building was restored at the end of the 19th century after being abandoned and partially destroyed.

The **Casa de Los Jesuitas** ★ (*Calle Las Damas*), made of brick and stone, is one of the oldest buildings in the city. Constructed by order of Nicolás de Ovando, it was given to the Society of Jesus in 1701. The Jesuits used the building as a college, which became a university in 1747. In 1767, when the Jesuits were expelled from the Dominican Republic, the house was taken over by the Spanish Crown.

The **Museo de Las Casas Reales** ★★ (*10 pesos; Tue to Sun 10am to 5pm; Calle Las Damas, at the corner of Calle Las Mercedes*) is located in two impressive palaces that originally housed the offices of royal institutions governing the territories, hence the name: museum of the "royal houses". The buildings were completed in the 1520s. Although they look fairly modest from the outside, their interior is richly decorated. Objects relating to the social, political, economic, religious and military history of the country are on display here. Among other things, there is a magnificent collection of weapons from different countries. The museum makes for an interesting visit, though not all rooms contain treasures.

At the end of Calle Las Damas stands the **Sundial** (*at the corner of Calle Las Mercedes*) built in 1753. This spot offers a splendid view of the port and the Río

Ozama. An extensive park can be viewed from here, which is slightly uninviting because of the lack of shade. A statue of Nicólas de Ovando stands at the center of the park and at the very end lies The **Alcázar de Colón** ★★★ (*20 pesos; Tue to Sun 9am to 5pm; Calle Las Damas at the far end of the park*). It dates from 1509-1510 and was built for Christopher Columbus' son, Diego Columbus, and his family. Diego Columbus succeeded Nicolás de Ovando as Viceroy of the colony in 1509. The beautiful façade, graced with 10 stone arches, looks out onto a large paved park where visitors will find a handful of benches and, in the center, a statue of Nicolás de Ovando. The Alcázar was abandoned for many years until architect Javier Borroso undertook reconstruction work in the 1950s. It has since been opened to the public.

Each room is decorated with beautiful period furniture, making this a visit not to be missed.

Near the Alcázar de Colón is the **gate** to the **Fuerte San Diego** (*Calle Las Damas*). Constructed in 1571, it served as the main entrance to Santo Domingo in the late 16th century. Part of the wall of the fortress that protected the city in the early colonial days can be seen here. Designed to face the river, this fortress was the main base of defense for the city.

At the edge of Parque Colón, follow the first little street on the right to reach **Calle Atarazana** ★ where, in 1509, the first group of shops in the New World was built. Visitors will find a row of small white houses with brick foundations, whose architectural style is unique in the country. Besides their architectural significance, they form a har-

Alcázar de Colón

monious ensemble, which still houses a few little shops to this day.

Double back to Calle Emilo Tejera and turn left on Isabel la Católica.

★

Calle Isabel la Católica

The architecture on Isabel la Católica is less harmonious than that on Calle Las Damas. There are, however, a few beautiful colonial buildings scattered among the much more recent additions.

The **Casa del Cordón** (*Calle Isabel la Católica, at the corner of Calle Tejera*), constructed in 1502, was one of the first stone residences in the New World. Upon arriving in 1509, Diego Colón lived here with his family before moving into the palace in 1510. The house is easy to spot, thanks to a large sculpted sash on the façade, the symbol of the Franciscan religious order.

The **Museo de Juan Pablo Duarte** ★ (*10 pesos; Mon to Fri 9am to noon and 2pm to 5pm, Sat and Sun 9am to noon; on Calle Isabel la Católica, at the corner of Calle Celestino Duarte*) is located in the house where Juan Pablo Duarte was born on January 26th, 1813. This national hero became famous as the leader of La Trinitaria, a secret organization that sought to liberate the Dominican Republic from Haitian domination. As a result of his efforts, the country declared independence on February 27th, 1844. Ousted from power, Duarte took exile in Venezuela, where he stayed until 1864, when Spain annexed the Dominican Republic (1861-1865). He returned to the Dominican Republic to oppose the Spanish takeover, but his efforts were in vain. Forced to leave the country again, he was never able to return and died in Carácas, Venezuela on July 15th, 1876. The museum highlights the important moments in his life, and displays many of his belongings. The building itself is unremarkable, but the exhibit is quite good.

The **Iglesia Santa Bárbara** and its connected **fort** (*Calle Isabel la Católica, at the corner of Avenida Mella*) erected in 1562, form a unique construction featuring elements from various architectural styles, including Gothic and baroque. The façade is distinguished by two square towers of different sizes and three brick arches at the entrance.

The fort was erected in the 18th century at a point

where the soldiers could keep an eye on a part of the city and on the Río Ozama. The church, for its part, constructed at the end of the 16th century, was destroyed by a hurricane a few years later. The sanctuary was then reconstructed and up to eight chapels have been designed here over the years.

After leaving the fort, take Calle Arzobispo Meriño to get to the Ermita San Anton.

Calle Arzobispo Meriño

After visiting the monastery, continue to Calle Hostos. A portion of the road is lined with pretty, colourful little houses.

The privately funded **Museo del Ámbar** ★ *(452 Arzobispo Meriño)* aims to educated the public about amber, the hardened sap of an extinct species of pine. It takes no more than 30mins to tour the museum, where you can learn about how amber was created and how insects and leaves were trapped in it. A number of fine specimens are displayed. Visitors will also have a chance to see amber of all different colours – not just yellow, but red, green and blue as well. The exhibit is also intended to help consumers learn to distinguish between real and imitation amber, and some useful tips are provided.

The **Ermita San Anton** *(Calle Hostos, at the corner of Calle Restauración)* is located just a few steps from the Monasterio San Francisco. Nicólas de Ovando had already planned the construction of this hermitage in 1502, but the building was not finished until 1586. A few years later, when the city was sacked by Drake, it was damaged in a fire. In 1930, after being entirely destroyed by a hurricane, the hermitage was reconstructed.

Built on a small hill in the heart of the old city, the **Monasterio de San Francisco** ★★ *(4 pesos; every day except Sun, 10am to 5pm; Calle Hostos, at the corner of Calle Tejera)* is impressive, though only ruins remain. Construction began in 1505 and the monastery was nearly completed during the 16th century, but in 1673, an earthquake completely destroyed it. Originally, it consisted of three distinct but connected buildings: the convent, the church and the chapel. The thick wall that surrounded the monastery still stands.

Among the ruins, the little chapel is the easiest building to identify, as its brick vault remains.

Soon after Santo Domingo was rebuilt on the right bank of the Río Ozama, Nicolás de Ovando ordered the construction of the **Hospital de San Nicolás** (*Calle Hostos, at the corner of Calle Mercedes; you will need to double back*) to provide care for the city's poor and needy. In ruins today, the building was shaped like a cross, a traditional Spanish design. It was surely the first hospital in the New World.

Parque Duarte is a little island of tranquillity, the perfect place to relax. It is beautifully landscaped and well worth a stop.

Dominating an entire side of the park, the **Imperial Convento de Santo Domingo** ★ (*Calle Hostos, at Calle Padre Billini*) is a magnificent stone structure that was built in several stages: the monastery itself dates from 1510, and the church from 1517 (though the original building was destroyed by an earthquake in the 16th century), both constructed in Gothic style. It encloses five chapels including the rosary chapel (1649) which is done in a 16th-century Spanish ornate architecture. The monastery also had the privilege of housing the first university in the Americas, **Universidad Santo Tomás de Aquino**. The building is still in good condition, but is scheduled for renovations and is thus closed to the public for the time being.

A few steps away from the convent, the Capilla de la **Tercera Ordén de los Dominicos** (*Calle Padre Billini, corner of Duarte*) dates from 1729 and served as the *Imperial Convento de Santo Domingo* in bygone days. It is adorned with a baroque façade and houses only one little nave in addition to its three small chapels.

At the Edge of the Colonial Zone

Located at the end of Calle El Conde, the **Parque Independencia** is surrounded by noisy, traffic-free streets, making it seem like an oasis of greenery and peace. A monument containing the tombs of three Dominican heroes who fought for the country's independence, Mella, Sanchez and Duarte, stands in the center of the park.

Sundays on Calle Mella once brought out droves of Dominicans to sample unique dishes prepared according to African culinary traditions. The street has changed considerably and is no longer an African neighbourhood, but a large commercial artery with countless shops selling all kinds of products.

The **Mercado Modelo ★** is also located here. Dominicans come to this enormous indoor market to sell foodstuffs, jewellery made of shells, larimar or amber, beachwear and crafts. This place is picturesque, but be careful (the aisles are narrow and sometimes dark) and always bargain before buying.

Plaza de la Cultura

The **Plaza de la Cultura** (*Calle Máximo Gomez, between Calles Cesar Nicola Penson and Pedro Henriquez Urena*), or cultural centre, includes four museums, the Museo de Arte Moderno, the Museo de Historia Natural, the Museo de Historia y de Geografía and the fascinating Museo del Hombre Dominicano. The Plaza also houses the Teatro Nacional.

The **Museo del Hombre Dominicano ★★** (*10 pesos; Tue to Sun 10am to 5pm*) is certainly the most interesting museum in Santo Domingo, if not the whole Dominican Republic. A rich collection of Taino art is displayed on the main floor. This indigenous people had already lived in the Dominican Republic for over a thousand years when Columbus arrived, and large numbers of them were wiped out during colonization. The entire ground floor of the museum is devoted to an exhibit of the art, religion and daily life of this society, which changed radically following the arrival of the Europeans. The few information panels in the museum are written only in Spanish.

The exhibits on the second floor retrace various events that have marked the colonization of the country. Many subjects are explored, and slavery is given special attention. The difficult living conditions faced by the thousands of Africans forced to come to the Dominican Republic are described. The last room houses a magnificent collection of carnival masks from different regions of the country.

The Carnival

Twice a year, in February and August, the carnival descends upon the Dominican Republic. The days leading up to and following this popular festival are animated with parades, large gatherings and dancing. The highlight of these wild festivities is unquestionably the carnival characters, dressed in brightlycoloured costumes and masks, which are often endowed with huge horns. Whether *diablos cojuelos* from Santo Domingo or La Vega, *lechones* from Santiago, *toros y civiles* from Monte Cristi, *papeluses* from San Francisco or *buyolas* from San Pedro de Macorís, these amusing devils roam the streets in search of sinners. Some of the masks are on display in the Museo del Hombre Dominicano in Santo Domingo (see p 108).

The carnival's origins are obscure, but celebrations such as these take place in a good number of Latin countries. They may be derived from a pagan ritual that once honoured the coming of spring and the rejuvenation of nature, or perhaps even from an ancient Roman festival. The fact remains that this celebration been kept alive through the ages and has adapted to each country's customs and traditions.

Excursion to Jarabacoa

Located in the mountains of the Cordillera Centrale, at an altitude of more than 500m, Jarabacoa is blessed with pleasant temperatures all year long. Many wealthy Dominicans have their second home here, and the attractive houses that line the streets give the city an affluent look. The lively downtown area features an attractive little park, beside which stands an elegant colonial-style church.

While the city has its appeal, visitors and artists are more often attracted to the rolling countryside surrounding it. The region is also renowned for horse breeding, and equestrian sports are very popular here. Golf, swimming at the foot of waterfalls and in *balnearios*, as well as a host of other sports activities visitors can be practised in the region, make Jarabacoa an increasingly popular holiday resort.

Rancho Baiguate, now a well known company, organizes several sport activities in the region such as river rafting.

El Salto de Jimenoa ★★ *($1; 10km from Jarabacoa on the way to La Vega, near the Alpes Dominicanos hotel, a road about 5km long leads to the entrance of the site, from there it is a 5min walk)* is one of the most beautiful waterfalls in the country. The water cascades down about 30m into a natural pool, perfect for swimming. The setting is idyllic. Footbridges lead up the river to the falls, and there is a little café that sells refreshments.

El Salto de Baiguate ★ *(free admission; heading to Constanza, take the third road to the right after the Pinar Dorada Hotel, after a few kilometres, you will see a parking lot; from there it's a 10min walk)* is not as spectacular a waterfall as the former, but is nonetheless very pretty. It, too, is about 30m high, with a natural pool at its base. The area, however, is less developed than Salto de Jimenoa.

The **Balneario de la Confluencia** *(at the end of Calle Norberto Tiburcio)*, at the confluence of the Jimenoa and Yaque del Norte rivers, is a tumultuous whirlpool where you can go swimming. There is a small park beside the balneario.

The **Balneario de la Guazaras** *(take Calle Norberto Tiburcio, then turn left on the third road after the fork)*, near the centre of Jarabacoa, is a waterfall and a popular swimming spot with the city's younger population.

Accommodations

When it comes to accommodations the choices are endless.

Room rates vary enormously depending what type of establishment you choose, from the smallest hotel to the resort complex. Every room is subject to the 5% tax and the 6% service charge, however. It is customary to leave an extra 10 to 15 pesos per day for the room cleaning services; this can be left at the end of your stay. Most large hotels accept credit cards, while smaller hotels usually do not.

Types of Accommodation

Hotels

There are three categories of hotels. The low-budget places near the downtown areas offer only the basics in comfort. The rooms generally have a small bathroom and an overhead fan.

Medium-budget hotels typically offer simple air-conditioned rooms that are reasonably comfortable. These can usually be found in resort towns and larger cities.

Finally, there are the luxury hotels, found in resort towns and on large, secluded properties or in tourist areas. They all try to surpass each other in comfort and luxury. Several hotels in this last category belong to international hotel chains like Occidental Hoteles, LTI, Caribbean Village, Riv, Barcelo, Alegro, Marriott, Jack Tar Village and Sheraton.

Except for budget hotels, most places have their own generator, as power cuts are frequent in the Dominican Republic. Security guards keep watch over medium- and high-priced hotels.

Some hotels offer all-inclusive packages, which usually include two or three meals a day, all locally produced drinks (such as rum and beer), taxes and the service charge. When a package deal is available, it will be indicated next to the room rate in the hotel listings.

Apart-hotels

Apart-hotels offer all the services of a hotel, but each room has an equipped kitchenette. This is the most economical option for longer stays in the Dominican Republic.

Cabañas

This type of accommodation is only slightly different than a hotel. *Cabañas* offer rooms in separate little buildings. They are usually inexpensive, and some are equipped with kitchenettes.

Bed and Breakfasts

Some people have adapted their homes to receive guests. However, the level of comfort varies greatly from one place to another. Generally, guests do not have a private bathroom.

Youth Hostels

There are no youth hostels in the Dominican Republic, but many of the country's small hotels offer very good rates.

Puerto Plata

Puerto Plata has a fairly large network of accommodations. However, visitors wishing to stay near a beautiful beach often choose hotels outside of town, in Playa Dorada or in one of the many other resorts in the area. Keep in mind, though, that the big hotels in Puerto Plata often offer lower rates than those in Playa Dorada, and also provide efficient transportation to the best beaches in the region.

Several hotels downtown and near Long Beach offer accommodation suitable for those on a tight budget. Even so, Puerto Plata is not the best place on the northern coast for inexpensive lodging; Sosúa and Cabarete have a much better selection of hotels in this category.

The Hotel Dilone
$8

⊗
96 Calle 30 de Marzo
If you decide to stay in Puerto Plata anyway, the Hotel Dilone has rooms that are adequately comfortable.

El Indio
$20
⊗, ℜ
94 Calle 30 de Marzo
☎ *586-1201*
The El Indio Hotel has a few well-kept. rooms It is located on a quiet street in the heart of the town, and has a pleasant tropical garden. With no pool or beach nearby and no beach shuttle, this hotel is best suited to travellers with their own means of transportation. You can try negotiating the price of your room with the German-born owner.

Hostal Jimesson
$20

⊗
Calle John F. Kennedy, corner of Separación
☎ *586-5131*
Many historic houses still line the streets of Puerto Plata's old city, losing none of their charm to the passage of time. One of these enchanting dwellings is the Hostal Jimesson. Upon entering the main floor of this building, your gaze will inevitably be drawn to the many antiques that adorn each hall. As for the rooms, though lacking in beautiful period furniture, they are inviting and very well kept.

Camacho Hotel
$20
≈, ≡, ℜ
on the Malecón
☎ *586-6348*
For those with small budgets, The Camacho Hotel, facing the ocean on the *malecón*, is a good place to stay. Rooms are sparsely furnished, but clean and spacious.

Puerto Plata
$35
ℜ, ≈, ≡, ⊗
on the malecón
☎ *586-2588*
⇌ *586-8646*
The Puerto Plata is a new hotel on the *malecón*. At first sight, this little place is hardly charming, but its attractive secluded garden,

makes it a pleasant place to stay.

Puerto Plata Beach and Casino Resort
$180, all-inclusive
≡, ≈, tv, ℜ, ⊛, ♠
Malecón
☎ *320-4243*

The Puerto Plata Beach and Casino Resort is by far the most luxurious hotel complex in the city. Its excellent restaurants, beautiful gardens, casino, swimming pools and host of activities make it a wonderful place for a vacation. The nicely decorated rooms are clustered in small, pastel-coloured buildings, and they all have balconies. Shows are presented in the evenings, and everyday there is a shuttle to and from the main beaches of the area. It is best to reserve ahead of time during the winter months.

Playa Cofresí

Hacienda Resorts
all-inclusive
☎ *320-8303*
⇌ *320-0222*

One of the newest of the Dominican Republic's big hotel complexes stands at the edge of Playa Cofresí, just west of Puerto Plata. A veritable tourist village, the Hacienda Resorts are a cluster of no fewer than five hotels, each with its own distinctive features, designed to satisfy the widest possible range of expectations.

Garden Club
ℜ, ⊗

The Garden Club is made up of pretty buildings that are more like simple, comfortable little cottages than modern hotel rooms, lending this part of the complex an intimate atmosphere.

Elizabeth
≈, ⊗, ≡, ℜ

The Elizabeth, for its part, will appeal to visitors looking to stay in a lovely hotel that is small but still offers a high level of comfort and has a large, attractive garden. It is distinguished by its vaguely Spanish-style building, which has only 18 rooms but is quite charming.

Andrea
≈, ⊗, ≡, ℜ

The more modern-looking Andrea has two beautiful pools.

Tropical
≈, ⊗, ≡, ℜ

The choicest of the five hotels, The Tropical stands next to the beach. In addition to its splendid rooms and outstanding swimming pool, it boasts a lovely garden that opens onto Playa Cofresí.

Villas de Luxe
≈, ⊗, ≡, K

This is not really a hotel, but rather a heavenly little village with magnificent houses scattered across a vast, rolling stretch of land. The developers truly outdid themselves; the place has been designed so that each little house is isolated enough to ensure its occupants' privacy.

As the villas have only a few rooms each, a family can rent an entire one for themselves. Each has its own terrace with a magnificent view, a kitchenette and a private pool. A great deal of care has been taken with another important aspect of these all-inclusive hotels: the restaurants, which always serve a buffet with a good selection of delicious dishes. One last plus: all guests have access to the lovely Playa Cofresí.

Playa Dorada

All the hotels in Playa Dorada meet international standards. All have comfortable air-conditioned rooms, at least one pool, restaurants and dining rooms, bars and nightclubs, shops and sometimes a casino. Prices do not vary much from one hotel to the next, the most affordable being the **Heavens**, and the most expensive, the **Jack Tar Village**. Many hotels offer all-inclusive packages, that include three meals a day, all local beverages (Dominican beer, rum, etc.), taxes and service charges. If you arrive in Playa Dorada without a reservation, expect to pay an average of $110 per night (a bit less in the low season), or even more if you want to stay in a studio or deluxe apartment.

For stays of one week or longer, it is often much more economical to make reservations from home through a travel agent, as they often have discounts. Finally, remember that during the winter season there is always a risk that all of the hotels will be full.

Flamenco Beach Resort
all-inclusive
≡, ≈, ⊗, ℜ
☎ *320-6319*
≈ *320-6319*

The Flamenco Beach Resort is a large complex whose architecture has a certain Spanish feel to it. Guests stay in a series of white villas, with large balconies. The service is attentive and the fine woodwork in the lobby, bar, restaurant and elsewhere creates a warm, welcoming atmosphere. Guests have access to the beach.

ACCOMMODATIONS

1. Flamenco Beach Resort
2. Gran Ventana
3. Heavens
4. Jack Tar Village
5. Paradise Beach Club and Casino
6. Playa Dorada Hotel / Playa Naco Golf and Tennis Resort
7. Puerto Plata Village
8. Victoria
9. Villas Doradas

RESTAURANTS

1. Hemingway's Café

Playa Dorada

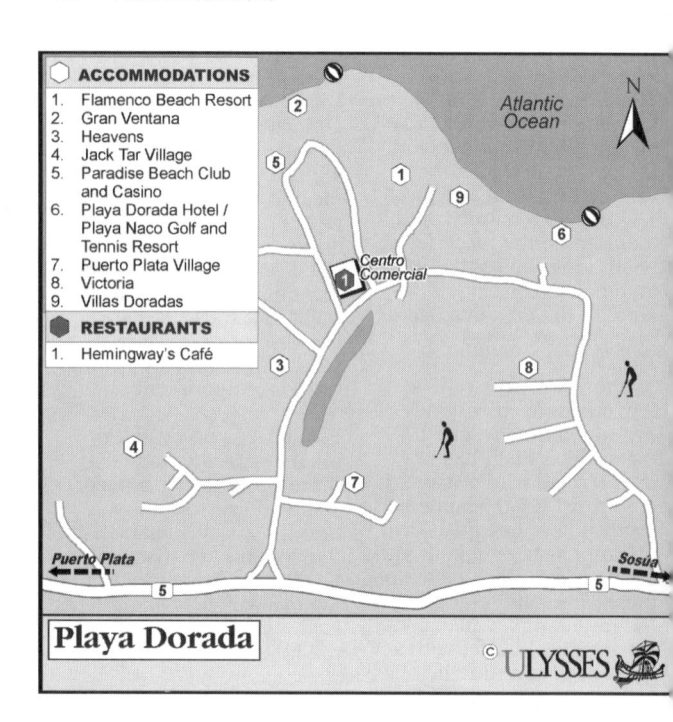

Heavens

all-inclusive

≡, ≈, ℜ, ⊗
☎ 562-7475
≠ 566-2436
≠ 566-2354

The Heavens Hotel Complex consists of two groups of buildings evidently built at different times. This is a pleasant place, even though some of the buildings are bunched together. The complex is near the golf course, and at a reasonable distance from the beach, which is accessible by way of a small path.

Jack Tar Village

all-inclusive

≡, ≈, ℜ, ⊗
☎ 320-3800
☎ 1-800-999-9182
≠ 320-4161

The Jack Tar Village occupies a large, well-maintained property. The rooms are set in charming villas arranged, like the name suggests, into a little village. The Jack Tar is especially popular with tennis players, as it has a large number of courts; it is also close to a golf course and the beach.

Many consider this the most luxurious hotel complex in Playa Dorada.

Paradise Beach Club and Casino
all-inclusive
≡, ≈, ℜ, ⊗, ♠
☎ *1-800-752-9236*
≈ *586-4858*

The Paradise Beach Club and Casino has a total of 436 units in several buildings decorated with attractive woodwork. The hotel's designers went to great lengths to make it visually pleasing; the impressive grounds feature luxurious gardens, waterfalls, ponds and swimming pools in interesting shapes. This unique and friendly resort offers comfortable rooms and lies right on the beach.

Playa Dorada Hotel
all-inclusive
≡, ≈, ℜ, ⊗, ♠
☎ *320-3988*
☎ *1-800-423-6902*
≈ *320-1190*

The Playa Dorada Hotel has 254 pleasantly decorated rooms, some with a clear view of the ocean. The nondescript older buildings of the hotel are located right on the beach. Guests will also find a casino, restaurants, a pleasant café and a piano-bar.

Playa Naco Golf & Tennis Resort
all-inclusive
≡, ≈, ℜ, ⊗
☎ *320-6226*
≈ *320-6225*

The Playa Naco Golf and Tennis Resort is graced with an imposing colonnaded façade and a monumental lobby overlooking a very large pool. The comfortable rooms are located in the building that surrounds the pool, where all the action takes place, and in various other structures scattered throughout the vast property. The Naco has several tennis courts, among other things.

Puerto Plata Village
all-inclusive
≡, ≈, ℜ, ⊗
☎ *320-4012*
≈ *320-5113*

The Puerto Plata Village is made up of charming little houses, some painted in pastel colours, others in bright colours, and all are equipped with balconies or terraces. The complex is pleasantly located in a large and airy garden, near the golf course and not too far from the beach. The service is excellent.

Villas Doradas
all-inclusive
≡, ≈, ℜ, ⊗
☎ *320-3000*
≠ *320-4790*

The Villas Doradas consists of a grouping of several-story buildings, each housing a few rooms with a balcony overlooking a large tropical garden. The lobby includes a relaxing open-air space with rattan chairs. A trail leads through a thicket, past a pond and on to the beach.

Gran Ventana
all-inclusive
≈, ≡, ℜ
☎ *412-2525*
≠ *412-2526*

The newest hotel in Playa Dorada, The Gran Ventana is a grand hotel complex whose buildings, all in warm hues, stand on a large piece of property by the sea. In the centre of this little village lies a huge swimming pool, the focal point of most of the day's activities. Great care has been taken with the decor, so all the rooms are spacious, have big picture windows and are adorned with lovely tropical colours. The restaurants of the Gran Ventura are known for the quality of their fare.

Victoria
all-inclusive
≈, ≡, ℜ
☎ *320-1200*
≠ *320-4862*

If you have no desire to spend your vacation in a place with a perpetually lively atmosphere, opt for The Victoria. This hotel cannot boast a seaside location, but offers a peaceful setting alongside a golf course. The building itself is sober-looking, as if to emphasize the establishment's desire to provide a tranquil atmosphere. Finally, many people claim that the food served here is among the best of any hotel in Playa Dorada.

Sosúa

Sosúa, which lives and breathes by tourism, offers accommodation for all budgets and tastes. Most of the hotels in the city are located in the El Batey neighbourhood, east of Playa Sosúa. None of these have direct access to Playa Sosúa, but they are all within walking distance.

Some hotels, however, face right onto smaller Playa Libre. Lodging is also available on the outskirts of Sosúa, in a few large complexes to the east and west of the city, along the ocean.

Sosúa 119

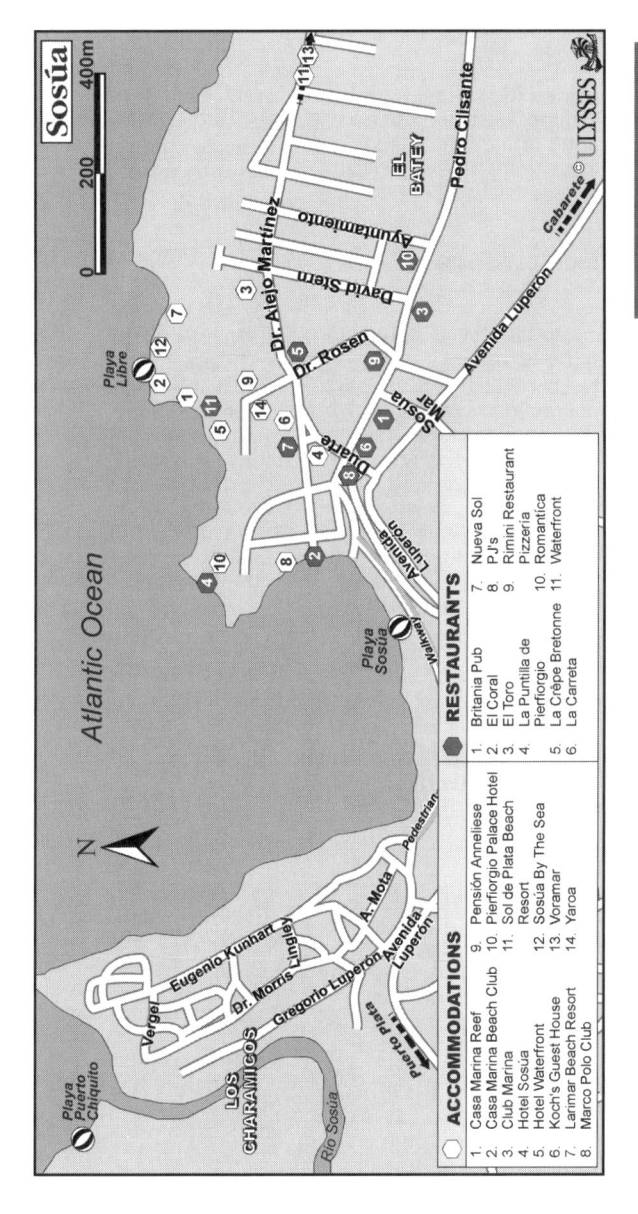

Accommodations

ACCOMMODATIONS

1. Casa Marina Reef
2. Casa Marina Beach Club
3. Club Marina
4. Hotel Sosua
5. Hotel Waterfront
6. Koch's Guest House
7. Larimar Beach Resort
8. Marco Polo Club
9. Pensión Anneliese
10. Pierfiorgio Palace Hotel
11. Sol de Plata Beach Resort
12. Sosua By The Sea
13. Voramar
14. Yaroa

RESTAURANTS

1. Britania Pub
2. El Coral
3. El Toro
4. La Puntilla de Pierfiorgio
5. La Crêpe Bretonne
6. La Carreta
7. Nueva Sol
8. PJ's
9. Rimini Restaurant Pizzeria
10. Romantica
11. Waterfront

During the summer, which is the off-season, when none of the hotels are filled to capacity, do not hesitate to negotiate for a better rate.

Koch's Guest House
$25
≡, K
close to Calle Martinez, El Batey
☎ *571-2284*

Koch's Guest House rents out clean *cabañas,* each with a kitchenette. The *cabañas* are scattered throughout a narrow well-maintained property, which ends at the ocean. The place may not be very luxurious, but it does offer reasonable rates and lots of peace and quiet, despite being located a few steps from the city's busiest streets. The owner can be a bit surly at times.

Pension Anneliese
$40
⊗, ℜ, ≈,
Calle Dr. Rosen, El Batey
☎ *571-2208*

The Pension Anneliese is a good, inexpensive little place with 10 spotless rooms, each with a balcony and a refrigerator. The rooms at the front boast a pretty view of the ocean, which is just a few metres away. The location is quiet, even though it's close to the heart of Sosúa. There is a pleasant pool in the little garden out back. Hearty and tasty breakfasts are served each morning *(starting at $3)*. The Pension Anneliese is run by a German couple that has lived in Sosúa for over 15 years.

Voramar
$35
ℜ, ≈, ⊗, ≡
at the east end of Sosúa
☎ *571-3910*
⇌ *571-3076*

Outside the centre of town, about 500m from the last buildings along Playa Libre, there are several inexpensive, well-kept and quiet hotels. One of these is The Voramar which has large, comfortable rooms, each with a balcony. A few hotels in the same category are located nearby, as are some narrow, sandy beaches. The Sosúa beach is just a few minutes' drive away.

Waterfront Hotel
$50
⊗, ≈, ℜ, ℝ
1 Calle Dr. Rosen, El Batey
☎ *571-2670*
⇌ *571-3586*

The Waterfront Hotel, also known as Charlie's Cabañas, rents out small white stucco cottages set in a garden by the ocean. Without being luxurious, this place is quaint and comfortable, and features a pleasant restaurant, a bar and a small pool. It is located right next to the Pension Anneliese and enjoys the same quiet atmosphere.

Sosúa

Sosúa Hotel
$45, bkfst
≡, ≈, ℝ, ℜ, *tv*
Alejo Martinez
☎ *571-2683*
☎ *571-3530*
≠ *571-2180*

The Sosúa Hotel is in a modern building located on a relatively hectic street in the centre of Sosúa. The rooms are pleasant and are equipped with a balcony or terrace.

Yaroa
$35
≡, ≈, ℜ
Calle Dr. Rosen
☎ *571-2651*
≠ *571-3814*

Situated on a quiet street, The Yaroa has the benefit of a tranquil location, though the decor of the rooms is somewhat time-worn.

Pierfiorgio Palace Hotel
≈, ≡, ℜ
☎ *571-2215*
≠ *571-2786*
www.pierfiorgio.com

Already reputed for the excellent setting of its restaurant, The Pierfiorgio is now acquiring a name for its recently erected Pierfiorgio Palace Hotel The rooms in this splendid, colonial-style edifice are spread out over two levels and all benefit from the long, stylish balconies that look out onto the sea. Rattan furniture and Haitian paintings embellish the ample and impeccable rooms that are also endowed with spacious bathrooms. Enclosing the hotel is a lovely garden dotted with some whirlpools in addition to a pool.

Sosúa by the Sea
$125, ½ b
≡, ≈, ℜ, *tv*
Playa Libre, El Batey
☎ *571-3222*
≠ *571-3020*

The Sosúa by the Sea is a comfortable, attractively decorated hotel complex overlooking a classic tropical garden, a pool and a restaurant with a beautiful view of the ocean. A wooden staircase leads down to the pretty Playa Libre, which is often much more relaxing than Playa Sosúa. The centre of Sosúa is only a few minutes away by foot.

Club Marina, **Casa Marina Beach Club** and **Casa Marina Reef Hotel** are all run by the same proprietor. Therefore, lodging at any one of the these three hotels will include access to the beach and the facilities of **The Casa Marina Beach Club**.

Club Marina
$120, all-inclusive
≡, ≈, ℜ, tv
Alejo Martinez
☎ 571-3939
⇄ 571-3110

The Club Marina is a pretty hotel with thirty comfortable, modern rooms and a swimming pool. This quiet place lies right next to Playa Libre, and just a few minutes' walk from Playa Sosúa.

Casa Marina Beach Club
$130, all-inclusive
≡, ≈, ℜ
Playa Libre, El Batey
☎ 571-3690
☎ 571-3691
☎ 571-3692
⇄ 571-3110

Among the most comfortable establishments in Sosúa, The Casa Marina Beach Club offers direct access to Playa Libre as well as well-maintained rooms, several of which boast ocean views. These are spread throughout a large complex consisting of several pastel-coloured buildings. The service is particularly attentive and professional. The Casa Marina is often booked solid in the winter; during the rest of the year, however, it is possible to negotiate the room rates.

Casa Marina Reef
$120
≡, ≈, ℜ
☎ 571-3690
⇄ 571-3110

A new addition to Sosúa, The Casa Marina Reef was erected next to the other two Marina properties. It is perched on top of some cliffs and offers a stunning view of the ocean below. Even from this height the beach is nearby since there is a short path that can take you there in no time. The architects' use of concrete is rather heavy-handed but the rooms provide exemplary comfort and a tasteful decor.

Marco Polo Club
$80
ℜ, ≈, ⊗, ≡, K, ⊛
at the end of Calle Alejo Martinez
☎ 571-3128
⇄ 571-3233

The Marco Polo Club, which enjoys an unimpeded view of Sosúa Bay, is a lovely little hotel built on a well laid-out piece of property along side a cliff. Though located almost right in the centre of town, it feels far from all the commotion.

Larimar Beach Resort
$90, bkfst
≡, ≈, ℜ, *pb, tv*
Playa Libre, El Batey
☎ *571-2868*
≈ *571-3381*
Also with direct access to the Playa Libre, The Larimar Beach Resort is a comfortable, modern hotel complex offering a range of services. Its several tall buildings are surrounded by a large garden of tropical plants and trees. Most rooms have a balcony or terrace.

Sol de Plata Beach Resort
$140, all-inclusive
≡, ≈, ℜ, *tv*
east of Sosúa
☎ *571-3600*
≈ *571-3380*
A few kilometres east of Sosúa, The Sol de Plata Beach Resort is an immense hotel complex where you can rent a room, a suite or a villa. The modern buildings face onto a private beach. A wide range of sports activities is organized here as well as evening shows, and a shuttle that takes guests to Sosúa and Cabarete.

Playa de Oro Hotel
$60
≡, ≈, ℜ, *tv*
☎ *571-0880*
≈ *571-0871*
This hotel offers accommodation in comfortable, more than adequate rooms. It stands on the beautiful white-sand beach between Cabarete and Sosúa.

Bella Vista
$90, all-inclusive
≈, ℜ, ≡
on the way to Cabarete
☎ *571-1878*
≈ *571-0767*
Right next to the Playa de Oro and in the same category, the Bella Vista offers all-inclusive packages. The rooms, each equipped with a balcony, are located inside two rows of rather simple-looking buildings. The back of the hotel looks right out onto the white-sand beach.

Punta Goleta Beach Resort
$180, all-inclusive
≡, ≈, ℜ
☎ *571-0700*
≈ *571-0707*
The Punta Goleta Beach Resort is a large, somewhat isolated hotel complex on the road between Sosúa and Cabarete. It offers all of the services one would expect from a luxury hotel – multiple restaurants and bars, a pool, sports and activities, shows, etc.
In order to offset the inconvenience of its isolation, a small bridge has been constructed which crosses the road.

Cabarete

Due to its growing popularity, Cabarete now offers a good selection of accommodations. Most of the hotels are of good quality, some offering greater luxury than others. If you visit Cabarete during the summer months, don't hesitate to look at several hotels and negotiate for the best price before making your choice.

Caribe Surf Hotel
$36
≈, ⊗, ℜ
☎ *571-0788*
⇌ *571-3346*
The Caribe Surf Hotel is built right on the beach, but at the east end of town, in the heart of a small residential neighbourhood removed from all the tourist activity. This is not a big, luxurious hotel complex, but rather a pleasant little inn with a great holiday-by-the-sea atmosphere. The rooms are very simply decorated but well kept and perfectly comfortable.

Albatros
$50
≡, ≈, K
on the way into town from the west
☎ *571-0841*
One of the first establishments on the way into Cabarete, The Albatros is a pretty hotel with a lovely tropical garden, in the middle of which lies a well-maintained pool. The rooms are well equipped, and complemented by natural lighting and a balcony or terrace. The Albatros was built quite recently.

Apart Hotel Cita del Sol
$60
≈, K, ⊗
in the centre of town
☎ *571-0720*
⇌ *571-0795*
The Apart Hotel Cita del Sol rents out clean but rather nondescript apartments that are spacious enough for families.

Villa Taïna
$65
≡
☎ *571-0722*
⇌ *571-0883*
Though the Villa Taïna, a charming little hotel of 16 rooms, is not directly on the oceanfront, it is, nevertheless a short walk away. What distinguishes this hotel is the quality of its rooms, which are stylishly decorated – in addition to being spacious and extremely well-maintained.

Windsurf Resort
$70
⊗, ≈, ℜ, ℝ, K
in the centre of town
☎ *571-0718*
⇌ *571-0710*
The Windsurf Resort rents out fully-equipped apartments.

Cabarete 125

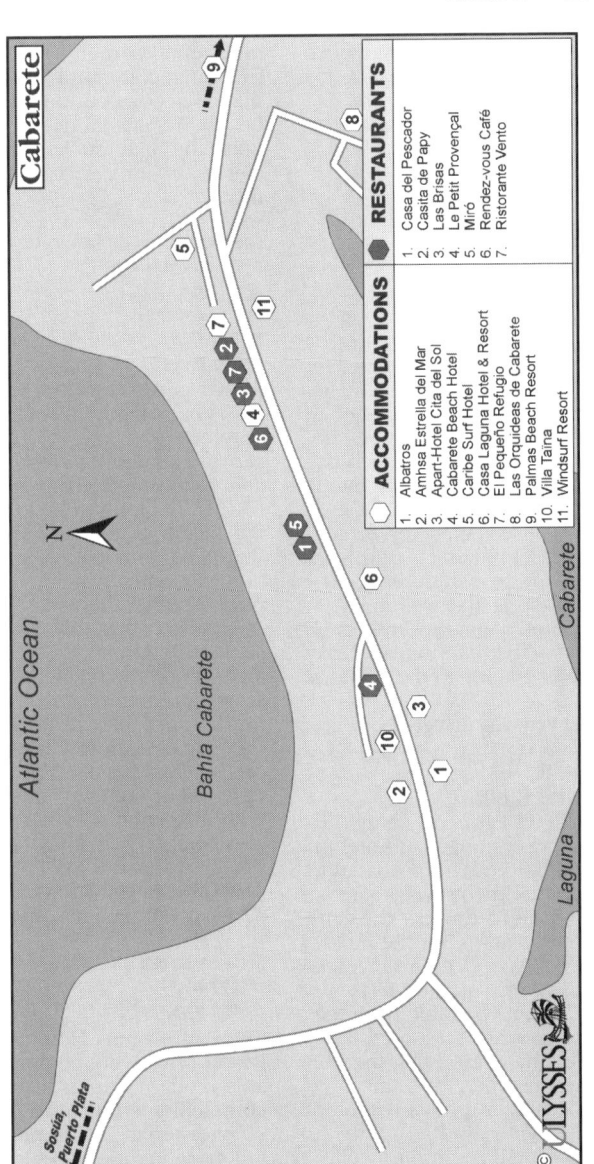

Cabarete

ACCOMMODATIONS

1. Albatros
2. Amnsa Estrella del Mar
3. Apart-Hotel Cita del Sol
4. Cabarete Beach Hotel
5. Caribe Surf Hotel
6. Casa Laguna Hotel & Resort
7. El Pequeño Refugio
8. Las Orquideas de Cabarete
9. Palmas Beach Resort
10. Villa Taina
11. Windsurf Resort

RESTAURANTS

1. Casa del Pescador
2. Casita de Papy
3. Las Brisas
4. Le Petit Provencal
5. Miró
6. Rendez-vous Café
7. Ristorante Vento

Accommodations

All of the rooms have been recently renovated. Weekly rates are available. The grounds include a pool where all sorts of activities are organized.

Cabarete Beach Hotel
$70
≡, ⊗
☎ *571-0755*
≠ *571-0831*

In the heart of town and directly on the water's edge is The Cabarete Beach Hotel, a handsome hotel of reliable comfort. At certain times of the day, it is busy with activity, but the intelligent arrangement of the premises helps you forget this. Other assets of this property include 24 commodious and well-maintained rooms sporting fairly attractive interiors and easy accessibility to the beach.

El Pequeño Refugio
$79, bkfst
≡, ℜ, ⊗
☎/≠ *571-0770*

The El Pequeño Refugio is another congenial hotel to note if you are prepared to abide downtown. Again, you need not fear the central location, for the buildings have been arranged so as to insulate guests as much as possible from the clamour of the street. It is for this reason that the rooms open onto the ocean, assuring a restful ambience and a superb view. All rooms are well-maintained and give access to a long, common balcony that also looks out onto the beach. A small garden provides the final touch to this already inviting environment.

Las Orquideas de Cabarete
$80, all-inclusive
⊗, ≈, ℜ
east of Cabarete
☎ *571-0787*
≠ *571-0853*

Las Orquideas de Cabarete offers reasonably priced, perfectly adequate accommodation in clean and comfortable rooms. Hidden behind the building is a beautiful tropical garden filled with lush vegetation around a swimming pool. Though the beach is only a short walk away, the setting is surprisingly quiet and will please those in search of tranquil surroundings. To get there, follow the little street a few hundred metres beyond the east end of the city. Suites with kitchenettes are also available.

Casa Laguna Hotel & Resort
$165, all-inclusive
≡, ≈, ℜ
in the centre of town
☎ *571-0725*
≠ *571-0704*

The Casa Laguna Hotel & Resort offers very comfortable modern studios, each complemented by a balcony or terrace. It is one of the more luxurious places in Cabarete, and despite its central location, it boasts a lovely natural ambience. Reserving in advance, especially in winter, is strongly recommended.

Las Palmas Beach Resort
$170
≈, ⊗, ℝ
☎ *571-0780*
⇌ *571-0781*

It goes without saying that downtown Carabete is fairly animated at times, but that is not to suggest that it is disagreeable. Still, some may prefer to lodge outside of downtown in order to be assured of a higher quality repose away from the bustle of Carabete. A good alternative is Las Palmas Beach Resort located about 1km east of the city. Situated directly on the beach, this resort consists of a dozen modern, two-storey buildings – all endowed with gardens. It houses rooms that are modestly decorated, but perfectly capable of satisfying a weary traveller's need for relaxation. Caution should be exerted when swimming along this part of the coast, as the undertow is particularly strong here.

Amhsa Estrella del Mar Hotel
$170
≡, ≈, ℜ
☎ *571-0808*
⇌ *571-0904*

The tourism development that Carabete has known over the last several years has favoured the emergence of hotel complexes that offer an all-inclusive format. The latest addition to this line of establishments is The Amhsa Estrella del Mar Hotel composed of a collection of several prominent buildings spread out in a vast garden that extends into a fine beach of white sand. Comprised of 164 ample rooms, which are modestly furnished and equipped with small balconies, this new member of the Amhsa chain has the blessing of a restful setting in the heart of downtown Cabarete.

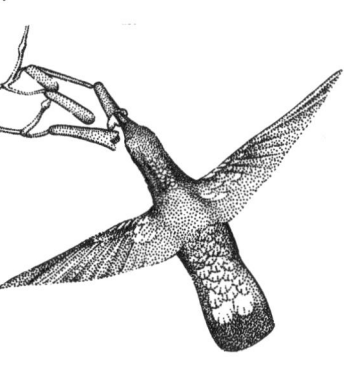

Río San Juan

Apart-Hotel San José
$14
⊗
facing the lagoon

The cheapest place to stay in Río San Juan is the Apart-Hotel San José whose rooms are very basic.

Río San Juan Hotel
$30
≡, ≈, ℜ
Calle Duarte
☎ 589-2379
☎ 589-2211
⇌ 589-2534

The Río San Juan Hotel stands on a large property right in the heart of town. The use of woodwork in the hotel's decor creates a warm atmosphere, and the gardens and the restaurant in the back are lovely. The rooms, while clean, are a bit stark. The Río San Juan has seen better days.

Bahía Blanca
$35
⊗, ℜ
Calle G.F. Deligne
☎ 589-2563
⇌ 589-2528

The Bahía Blanca is a veritable tropical paradise, and the choicest spot for a peaceful stay in Río San Juan. It is located on a quiet street just outside the centre of town, next to several small beaches.

The beautiful design of the Bahía Blanca allows for exceptional views of the ocean from the lobby, the restaurant and the terraces. Rooms are perfectly adequate. Because this is a small hotel, it is very peaceful and a convivial atmosphere prevails. Upon request, the hotel's staff can organize all sorts of excursions, like horseback riding, to help guests explore the region. It is also possible to rent smaller rooms (*$25*).

Bahía Principe
$180, all-inclusive
ℜ, ≈, ≡, ⊗
☎ 226-1590
⇌ 226-1994

The Bahía Principe stands at the edge of a magnificent, golden-sandy beach, which it has all to itself. Particular care has been taken with the layout, so not only do the rooms have all the comforts, but the setting is magnificent as well, making this a real little Caribbean paradise. The buildings are well maintained, the tropical garden is abloom with hundreds of flowers and guests receive a warm welcome. Even the little shopping gallery displays a remarkable attention to detail, with each shop set up inside a charming, brightly coloured little Creole cottage. The place is truly gorgeous.

Close-up of Santo Domingo's Panteon Nacional, a memorial to Dominican heros. - *Claude Hervé-Bazin*

The boutiques of Puerto Plata where jewellery, souvenirs and variety of other objects are found side by side.
- *T. Philiptchenko*

A symphony of colours and aromas on the streets of Puerto Plata.
- *T. Philiptchenko*

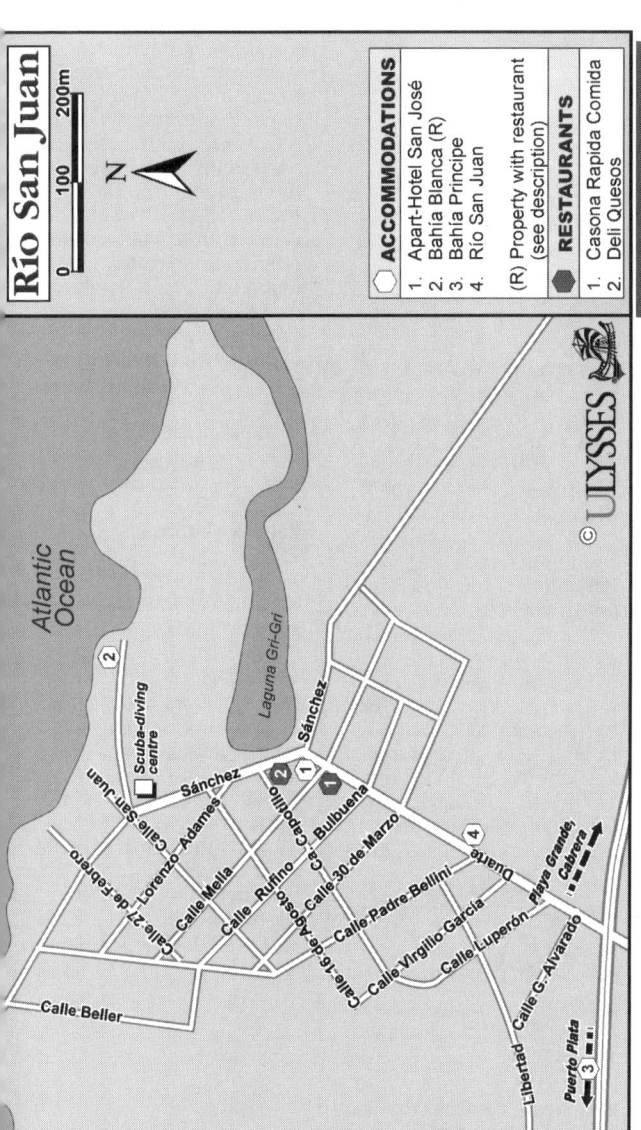

Playa Grande 129

Río San Juan

ACCOMMODATIONS
1. Apart-Hotel San José
2. Bahía Blanca (R)
3. Bahía Príncipe
4. Río San Juan

(R) Property with restaurant (see description)

RESTAURANTS
1. Casona Rapida Comida
2. Deli Quesos

Accommodations

Playa Grande

Caribbean Village
$190, all-inclusive
≈, ≡, ℜ
☎ *582-1170*
⇌ *582-6094*

The Caribbean Village is a large hotel complex located near the superb Playa Grande, one of the most idyllic beaches in the country. Several large buildings house comfortable, modern and spacious rooms, each of which has a balcony. Those at the back boast a magnificent view of the ocean. The Caribbean has tennis courts, a lovely pool, restaurants, bars and a dance club, and guests can enjoy a variety of sports activities, excursions and evening shows. A stairway leads from the complex to the beach, where a pleasant bar-restaurant has been built. The all-inclusive package offered by the Caribbean Village includes three meals and all local drinks.

Cabrera

La Catalina
$60
K, ⊗, ℜ, ≈
towards Cabrera
☎ *589-7700*
⇌ *589-7550*

Set back a bit from the road to Cabrera, on a hillside with a far-off view of the ocean, is La Catalina, a wonderful inn surrounded by magnificent tropical gardens. Beautiful vistas and a refreshing breeze create an enchanting ambience on the terrace of the dining room, which serves first-class cuisine. This elegant little complex offers well-maintained and beautifully furnished rooms, as well as one- and two-bedroom apartments. Guest can reach the neighbouring beaches and villages by taxi.

Nagua

Hotel Carib Caban
$25
⊗, ℜ
less than 10 km from Nagua on the way to Samaná
☎ *543-6420*
⇌ *584-3145*

Nagua has a limited choice of accommodations, so if you decide to spend more than a day in the region, it is better to stay on the outskirts of town, on the road towards the Samaná Peninsula. The Hotel Carib Caban has small, fairly well-kept rooms and villas overlooking a quiet, undeveloped beach.

Restaurants

There is something for every taste from little cafeterias serving local inexpensive dishes to gourmet restaurants offering refined fare.

The choice is particularly varied in Santo Domingo and near the resort areas. Elsewhere, however, often the choice is limited to local specialties. Service is usually friendly and attentive in both small and large restaurants. An 8% tax and 10% service charge are added to every bill.

Dominican Cuisine

Only slightly spicy, Dominican cuisine is above all simple and nourishing, as it is prepared from local ingredients. Dishes usually consist of meat, fish, chicken or seafood accompanied by rice, beans or plantain. By visiting a few local restaurants you will certainly have the chance to enjoy some local specialties like *mondongo, asopao* or *sancocho*.

Drinks

There are a few local Dominican beers, including Quisqueya, the new Soverana and El Presidente. All three are of export quality, though the most popular is El Presidente.

Most hotels and restaurants also serve imported beers.

Wine is not very popular in the Dominican Republic, and little is produced locally. The imported wines served in restaurants are often quite expensive – particularly the French ones. We would advise you to try one of the Chilean wines, which deliver good quality for the price.

Rum, whether golden, white, dark or aged, whether served as an aperitif or digestif, is definitely the most sought after alcohol. Sold everywhere (it is sometimes easier to find than bottled water), rum has been close to the hearts of all Dominicans since sugar cane has been grown here, and grown well, we might add. Do not miss the chance to savour some Brugal Extra Viejo or Ron Bermúdez.

Puerto Plata

Puerto Plata has a wide selection of restaurants to suit all budgets and all palates. The best ones are found mainly in the hotel zone. There are, however, a host of small restaurants in the downtown area that serve simple, inexpensive food. In the evening, the promenade along the ocean is lined with food stalls selling light meals and sweets.

Helado Bon
$
at the corner of Calles Separación and Beller

For a refreshing break while strolling through the streets of Puerto Plata, ice cream is just the thing, and Helado Bon, located right in front of Parque Duarte, is just the place to get it. This neighbourhood also has several other little restaurants.

Plaza Cafe
$
on Calle 30 de Marzo near Calle Beller

A small restaurant with a pleasant atmosphere, the Plaza Cafe specializes in *pica pollo* and fish. It has an open-air terrace alongside a quiet street.

Portofino
$$
Avenida Mirabal

The Portofino, located in the hotel zone, is an attractive restaurant ensconced in greenery. The menu consists essentially of pizzas and other well-prepared Italian dishes. There is an outdoor terrace looking onto the street, as well as an indoor dining room.

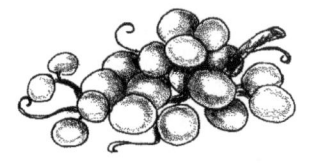

Here is a short food glossary to help you understand Dominican menus:

Agua	water
Ajo	garlic
Almuerzo	lunch
Asopao	a tomato-, rice-, seafood- or fish-based dish
Arroz	corn
Batida	a fruit juice made with ice and milk
Camarones	shrimps
Carne	meat
Carne de res	beef
Cena	supper
Cerveza	beer
Chichearón	cooked marinated chicken or beef
Chivo	kid
Chuleta	cutlet
Conejo	rabbit
Desayuno	breakfast
Empanadas	small pastries filled with meat or vegetables
Filete	steak filet
Granadilla	grenadine
Habichuela	plate of beans
Habichuela con dulce	sweet red beans (during the week of Easter only)
Huevo	egg
Jalao	coconuts and molasses
Jamón	ham
Jugo	juice
Lambi	small mollusks (also called Lambis in English)
Langosta	lobster
Leche	milk
Limón	lemon
Mangu	green bananas and meat
Mariscos	seafood
Masitas	coconut powder and brown sugar

Mermelada	preserve
Mofongo	ripe bananas with grilled sesame
Mondongo	tripe
Naranja	orange
Pan	bread
Papas fritas	fried potatoes
Postulad	wheat pancake filled with seafood, meat or vegetables
Pescado	fish
Pica pollo	fried chicken
Piña	pineapple
Plátanos fritos	fried bananas
Pollo	chicken
Postre	dessert
Queso	cheese
Sancocho	meat dish boiled with vegetables
Sopa	soup
Tamarindo	tamarin
Tortilla	omelette
Tostada	toast
Vino	wine
Zanahoria	carrot

Neptune
$$$
inside the Puerto Plata Beach and Casino Resort Hotel Complex
The Neptune is the most popular restaurant in Puerto Plata for fish and seafood. The atmosphere is relaxed and cosy, and the service, excellent.

Jarvis
$-$$
Malecón, corner of José R. López
☎ *320-7265*
Benefiting from a privileged position on the *malecón*, the Jarvis is an ideal spot for those looking for a light meal: sandwiches and pizzas are prominently featured on the menu. Meals are served on a terrace covered with a canopy of local palm leaves in a peaceful spot nestled away from the noise of the street.

Polanco
$$
25 John F. Kennedy
☎ *586-9174*
Polanco, an intimate and congenial restaurant, has

carved its reputation from the quality of the seafood dishes that it offers at unbelievably affordable prices (of particular note is the rock lobster). A palm-roofed patio and a salutary service top the bargain off with a certain charm.

La Ponderosa
$$-$$$
156 Calle 12 de Julio
☎ **586-1597**

Noted for the quality of its Dominican specialties as well as for its delectable fish and seafood dishes, La Ponderosa is bound to awaken your appetite. Considered one of Puerto Plata's gems, this little bistro, enhanced with a cute outside patio, exudes a contagiously casual spirit.

Playa Dorada

The vast majority of restaurants in Playa Dorada are located in the hotels. A wide variety of international cuisine is available, as well as excellent local dishes. Make sure to try the Dominican cuisine, which is generally delicious and only mildly spicy. Light, inexpensive dishes can be found at the Playa Dorada Plaza, and at the snack bars in most hotels.

Hemingway's Café
$-$$
Plaza Dorada
☎ **320-2230**

For burgers, steaks, fajitas, pasta, salads and other simple fare, head to Hemingway's Café, which has a young, convivial atmosphere. On weekends, in the evening, you can dine to the sounds of live pop music.

Sosúa

Over the years, Sosúa has seen the opening of a plethora of restaurants for all tastes and budgets. If you want a quick bite to eat, countless stalls up and down the beach sell refreshments and fish and chicken snacks, plus a variety of other simple dishes. There are also several little restaurants on Calle Dr. Rosen in the El Batey neighbourhood, which, like those in the hotels, offer mostly affordable international cuisine.

La Crêpe Bretonne
$-$$
Calle Dr. Rosen

La Crêpe Bretonne serves a selection of dinner and dessert crepes. This little place, with about 10 tables under a palm-thatched roof, is good for a quick snack or a light evening meal.

PJ's
$-$$

You'll feel more like you are in the United States than the Caribbean at PJ's, but this is still a neat place for an evening drink and a burger or some other American fast food specialty. The atmosphere is friendly, and the decor does have a certain something.

Rimini Restaurant Pizzeria
$-$$

Situated on the second floor of a small house with a palm roof, The Rimini Restaurant Pizzeria offers an inexhaustible assortment of pizzas, or, if you prefer, a healthy plate of pasta.

Britania Pub
$$

Pedro Glissante

If you are one of those people who think that there's nothing like a good cold beer after a day in the sun, head to the Britania Pub, where they also serve good steak and shrimp.

La Carreta
$$

Pedro Clisante
☎ *571-1217*

La Carreta is another establishment whose menu is brimming with a variety of dishes that, as the name suggests, have an Italian focus. One can count on spending an animated evening here in the dining room that opens out onto one of Sosua's most popular streets, making for an excellent vantage point from which to survey the comings and goings of the city.

El Coral
$$

at the end of Calle Alejo Martinez

The menu at the El Coral places special emphasis on Dominican specialties and seafood. Hearty servings of tropical fruit are served for breakfast, and at lunch there is a selection of simple dishes. The terrace, located atop a promontory, offers a striking view of the bay of Sosúa.

Romantica Restaurant
$$

David Stern
☎ *571-2509*

The Romantica Restaurant, warmly decorated in an orangehue with tiled floors and enchanting furnishigs is bound to please everyone. The comprehensive menu includes rock lobster, fish, steak, pasta, pizza, in addition to some Italian and German culinary specialties; in short, something for everyone.

Waterfront
$$

Calle Dr. Rosen in the Waterfront Hotel

The menu at The Waterfront includes both light meals and more sophisticated local and international specialties. Once a week, there is an inexpensive all-you-can-eat barbecue. This is a pleasant spot with a beautiful ocean view. It becomes a quiet bar towards the end of the evening.

El Toro Restaurant
$$-$$$
David Stern

Even under the hot Caribbean sun one can be overcome with a craving for a tender and juicy steak. If this is something that happens to you, head straight for The El Toro Restaurant where succulent steaks can be savoured in a stylish dining room that opens out onto the thoroughfare. Open in the evenings only.

La Puntilla de Pierfiorgo
$$-$$$
1 Calle La Puntilla
☎ *571-2215*

Every visitor should dine at the La Puntilla at least once. It has been one of the most prestigious establishments in Sosúa for several years, known not only for its excellent Italian cuisine but also for its splendid location. Its multi-level balconies overhanging the waves offer the most spectacular view in Sosúa. The dishes, mostly Italian and seafood, are all finely prepared and delicious. To enjoy the breathtaking setting at its best, try to arrive just before sunset.

Cabarete

Cabarete has a vast array of restaurants in all price ranges. A good number of restaurants on the beach offer inexpensive meals, perhaps because so many young windsurfers come to Cabarete. There are some more elaborate dining possibilities here as well.

Rendez-Vous Café
$
in the centre of town

The Rendez-Vous Café is a friendly place to relax for a drink or a light meal.

Las Brisas Restaurant
$-$$
on the main street
☎ *571-0708*

A palm-thatched roof, a smattering of tables, and the sea for as far as the eye can see, compose the setting of the Las Brisas Restaurant. Here, the best way to relish one of the savoury dishes, whether it be a seafood, beef brochette, or spaghetti platter, is with your feet in the sand. The ambience, which is casual and congenial, becomes a little livelier at night when the restaurant is transformed into a bar.

Miró
$-$$

The quintessentially charming café, Miró, hides behind the façade of a pretty little hut where murals inspired by Juan Miró have been painted. It makes for a memorable introduction to this oceanfront café with an unpretentious menu that highlights salads, pizzas, and pasta.

Casa del Pescador
$$-$$$
on the main Street

The menu at the Casa del Pescador naturally spotlights fish and seafood. The food is exquisite and the charming beach-side location is propitious to long relaxed meals. Be sure to try the daily special.

Casita de Papy
$$-$$$

Tucked on the first floor of a small cabin, Casita de Papy is a restaurant that brings together simplicity and charm. It manages to instill a friendly atmosphere perfect for holiday dining on the beach, with only the help of a few tables, a ceiling fan, and, of course, the view of the beach. The ocean theme carries on to the menu which consists of seafood, rock lobster, and shrimp. Reservations are necessary but you'll need to drop by during the afternoon, since Papy doesn't have a telephone.

Le Petit Provençal
$$-$$$
west entrance at Cabarete

Le Petit Provençal provides a welcome change of pace. The French proprietor welcomes patrons at the door, and generally manages the restaurant. In the kitchen, the chef creates day after day some of the most beloved delicacies of France. Kidneys in mustard sauce, ribs with *roquefort* and *ceps*, fresh fish, and rock lobster might be available while you're there. Always delicious, the food is the main star, but the laid-back and hospitable ambience ranks not far behind, made up of a simple décor of plastic chairs and wooden tables.

Ristorante Vento
$$-$$$
on the main street

In the heart of the city, Ristorante Vento promises delectable Italian fare, from succulent pasta dishes and salads, all the way to carpaccio. The ambient combination of the waning daylight and comfy seating by the ocean will only heighten your dining experience. The restaurant is only open for dinner.

Río San Juan

Most of the restaurants in Río San Juan are on Calle Duarte and along the shores of the lagoon. Generally, the cuisine is simple and good. For more sophisticated fare, try the restaurants in the hotels.

Casona Rapida Comida
$
Calle Duarte, opposite the Brigandina

Located in a pretty little pastel-coloured house, The Casona Rapida Comida serves fast-food, including great empanadas (*less than $1*).

Quesos Deli
$
facing the lagoon

Well-located in front of the lagoon, The Quesos Deli is a small eatery serving sandwiches and other simple dishes that are ideal after a boat trip.

Bahía Blanca
$$
Calle G.F. Deligne
☎ *589-2563*

The dining room in the Hotel Bahía Blanca is an idyllic spot to enjoy a good meal while taking in the sunset from the terrace overlooking the ocean. The menu includes meat, fish and seafood prepared according to local and international recipes. Professional service.

Río San Juan
$$$
Calle Duarte
☎ *589-2211*

The restaurant in the Río San Juan Hotel enjoys an excellent reputation in the area for its local cuisine. A footbridge leads to the restaurant, which stands on stilts overlooking a garden. Evening shows are occasionally presented.

Cabrera

La Catalina
$$-$$$
before Cabrera

Whether you are staying in town or just passing through, be sure to stop for a bite at the restaurant in the La Catalina Inn. Savoury and well-presented light meals are served at lunchtime, while a gourmet French menu is offered in the evening. The setting is enchanting and boasts a lovely view of the ocean.

Making Rum

Sugarcane has been grown in the Dominican Republic for centuries, long requiring hard labour on the part of local men and women, especially at harvest time. The men were responsible for cutting each plant down to the soil, stripping off the leaves (for fodder) and cutting each cane into one-metre-long pieces. The women followed, tying up the pieces into bundles of 10 to 12 pieces. This work was labour-intensive and was carried out under the hot sun. Although harvesting sugar cane is somewhat easier today thanks to modern equipment, it is still an arduous task.

After being tied into bundles, the sugarcane is taken to the factory so that its juice can be extracted. When pressed the first time, it produces a substantial quantity of juice. To collect the remaining liquid, the cane is moistened with water, and then pressed a second time. The crushed fibres, called *bagasse*, become fuel for the mill, while the sweet juice is used to make a variety of other products, notably sugar and rum.

The sweet juice (molasses) is fermented to produce a liquid with an alcohol content of 95%, which is then diluted with distilled water in copper barrels. The alcohol is then decanted into another set of copper barrels and sometimes mixed with almonds or caramel to give it its characteristic flavour and colour. This blend is decanted yet again, this time into wooden barrels and aged for one to 25 years. Afterward, it is filtered and sampled, then left to settle for 15 days in copper barrels to make sure there will be no sediment in the finished product. Finally, the rum is bottled, thus becoming the favourite companion in both the joy and sorrow of the Dominican population.

Santo Domingo

You will find a good place for lunch among the restaurants that line the pedestrian street, El Conde. We suggest one of these:

Barriloche
$
Calle El Conde near Duarte
This restaurant is very popular with Dominicans at lunchtime. The cafeteria-style layout is quite simple; choose your meal at the counter, and sit down to eat it in the large nondescript room with the television. This place is ideal for a filling, inexpensive meal (*pollo, arroz* and *habichuela*).

Cafe de Las Flores
$
Calle El Conde near Sanchez
Continuing along the pedestrian street, El Conde, the Cafe de Las Flores is an unpretentious establishment that offers mainly Dominican food. There are also a few Italian and international dishes on the menu. On the terrace you can watch the hustle and bustle of town while listening to the latest *merengue* and *bachata* hits.

L'Avocat
$$
Calle El Conde
☎ *688-1068*
L'Avocat is one of the most pleasant areas of the Colonial Zone, between Las Damas and Isabel la Católica. The restaurant serves delicious fish and seafood dishes, as well as chicken and steak. Try to get a seat in the courtyard in back of the restaurant; it is very quiet there but there are only three tables.

La Crêperie
$$
Calle Atarazana
Plaza de España
☎ *221-4734*
Right opposite the Alcazar de Colomb, on the Plaza de España, La Crêperie serves sandwiches and salads, as well as excellent crêpes. The shaded terrace on Plaza de España is a good place to go when it gets hot, especially at midday. It is also possible to sit in the small dining room located on the other side of Calle Atarazana.

Meson de la Cava
$$$
Avenida Mirador del Sur
☎ *533-2818*
Meson de la Cava is definitely one of the most well known places in Santo Domingo, and merits a visit if only to admire its originality. Indeed, like its name indicates, the Meson de la Cava was built inside a large cave and the setting is spectacular. Of course, prices are high and the place is mostly frequented by tourists who come for

the Dominican and international specialities.

Ristorante La Briciola
$$$
152-A Arzobispo Meriño
☎ **688-5055**
By far the most beautiful restaurant and one of the best places to eat in Santo Domingo, the Ristorante La Briciola is just the place for special occasions. Here you can savour Italian specialities prepared with flair, which are served in an elegant dining room or better yet, under the stars in a magnificent interior courtyard surrounded by brick arches. The design of the place is absolutely magnificent. It is better to make reservations on weekends.

Jarabacoa

Don Luis
$$
next to Parque Duarte
The Don Luis is well-located right in the heart of town, near Parque Duarte. It is a pleasant spot, but can get noisy. The menu consists mainly of steak and chicken prepared in a variety of ways. Great ice cream is available next door.

Entertainment

Nocturnal life along the coast has everything to please those in a festive mood, from lively Dominican dance clubs and electrifying mega-clubs at the large hotel complexes to quieter establishments where you can have a glass of wine while looking at the ocean.

Puerto Plata

Among the more pleasant districts for an evening stroll is the *malecón*, the boardwalk that runs along the ocean for several kilometres. In the evening, many Dominican families and couples take walks there, livening this part of town up a little. Many stalls are set up on the sidewalk where you can buy food.

Playa Dorada

Playa Dorada has an active and varied nightlife centred around the big hotels, almost all of which have at least one bar and often a dance club and a casino as well. Local performers and groups often perform at the hotels. As the schedules and type of entertainment vary, it is best to check what's on when you arrive.

If the evenings seem a little long to you, you can go to **The Plaza Dorada Cinema**, which shows movies in English every night.

Sosúa

The choice of bars and cafes is never-ending in Sosúa, and includes the pleasant and friendly **Waterfront** (*in the hotel of the same name*), where you can listen to some jazz while imbibing local or imported drinks.

The **Tall Tree**, another pleasant spot is on crowded, noisy Calle Pedro Glissante. Located on the main floor of a small house that opens out onto the street, it is the perfect place to sip a drink while studying the behaviour of the many passers by.

Most of the restaurants in Sosúa become terrace bars as the evening wears on; one of the liveliest is always **PJ's** (*Calle Pedro Glissante*).

If you feel like dancing, most of the dance clubs are located in the heart of Sosúa on Calle Pedro Glissante and Dr. Rosen.

Cabarete

Before heading out to dinner, catch a few drinks in the setting sun at one of the many restaurants on the beach.

The place to be for cocktails is none other than **Onno's Bar**, right on the beach, from late afternoon to late at night. A smallish house shelters a few tables and a long counter. There are live bands playing on some nights. Río San Juan

The little **Gri-Gri Discotheque** on Calle Sanchez, right near the lagoon, is generally open weekend evenings. Though slightly more touristy, **Méga Disco** will fulfill those looking for a party, awesome music and dancing.

For a quieter evening, try the **Hotel Río San Juan Piano Bar**, which has regular shows in the evenings.

Shopping

Boutiques in Puerto Plata, Sosúa and Cabarete sell all kinds of merchandise, most notably cotton clothing and local crafts such as wooden sculptures, mahogany boxes and folk-art paintings, as well as beautiful amber, shell and larimar jewelry.

Delicious and inexpensive rum, coffee and cigars are also good choices.

Opening Hours

Most stores are open from 9am to 5pm. Stores rarely close at lunchtime, especially in resort areas.

Alcohol

Alcohol, most often rum and beer, is sold in all convenience stores (*mercados*).

Mercados

You can buy all kinds of things in these little grocery stores, including food, beauty products, alcohol and cigarettes.

Puerto Plata

In addition to the shops in the large hotels, many places downtown sell souvenirs, jewellery and clothing.

The busiest commercial streets are Calles J.F. Kennedy and 12 de Julio, near the central park.

One of the best places to buy local crafts and jewellery is the gift shop at the **Museo del Ámbar** (*at the corner of Prudhomme and Duarte*).

Playa Dorada

The **Plaza Dorada** has all sorts of little shops selling rum, cigars, compact discs, jewellery, bathing suits and beachwear. The merchandise is generally of good quality, but the prices are a tad higher than elsewhere in the country. Boutiques can also be found inside many of the hotels.

Sosúa

Sosúa is certainly not lacking in stores, which are located downtown, mostly on Calles Pedro Glissante and Alejo Martinez, and along the beach. You will find souvenirs, clothing, local and Haitian paintings, sculptures, etc. Prices are negotiable in many of these places.

There are numerous small shops in the village, some selling jewelry made of silver, shells, amber, or larimar. If your pocket book permits, head to **Harrison's** (*corner of Clisante and Dr. Rosen*) where you are bound to find some beautiful gold pieces, though at much higher prices. You can stock up on Dominican cigars of all sizes and all aromas at **Sosúa Cigar Discount** (*in front of the Sosúa-by-the-Sea Hotel*).

The Family Jewel Shop on Pedro Glissante is a good place for jewellery, and also sells amber pieces at reasonable prices.

Cabarete

If you're in the market for lovely local handicrafts or pretty jewellery, **Atlantis** ☎ *571-2286* is one of the best shops in town.

Harrison's jewelry boutique has also opened its doors in Cabarete, and proudly displays a few of its creations in gold and precious stones. They also carry some magnificient amber and larimar jewelry.

The **Carib Bic Center** not only rents out sailboards, but also has a small shop that carries nice sports clothes as well as some windsurfing equipment.

Dominican Tobacco and Cigars

Although the cigar-making industry in the Dominican Republic is not as old or as large as Cuba's, it produces some of the finest cigars in the world by such famous brand-names as Davidoff, Juan Clemente, and Arturo Fuente. Dominican cigars are much appreciated by aficionados.

The cigar was invented in Seville in 1676 and was made entirely out of tobacco. In the next few centuries, many cigar factories were established throughout Europe, but the quality of the cigars was limited, because it took a long time to ship the tobacco leaves from Caribbean plantations. Finally, in the late 19th century, some producers in Cuba began to open factories near their plantations, significantly improving the quality of the cigars. This is how Cuban cigars came to be famous all over the world. When Fidel Castro nationalized the cigar industry, some producers decided to move their factories to the neighbouring Dominican Republic, mostly around Santiago. Therefore, for the last 10 years, Davidoff cigars, one of the most renowned brands in the world, have been made exclusively in the tiny republic.

Some highly-recommended Dominican cigars:

Double R and Special T by Davidoff
Churchill, Obelisco and Rothschild by Juan Clemente
No 9 by Avo
Rothschild by Canaria d'Oro
Gran Corono by Montesino
Pythagoras and Magnificat by Credo
Briva Fina and Briva Conserva by Henry Clay

Glossary

GREETINGS
Goodbye	*adiós, hasta luego*
Good afternoon and good evening	*buenas tardes*
Hi (casual)	*hola*
Good morning	*buenos días*
Good night	*buenas noches*
Thank-you	*gracias*
Please	*por favor*
You are welcome	*de nada*
Excuse me	*perdone/a*
My name is...	*mi nombre es...*
What is your name?	*¿cómo se llama usted?*
no/yes	*no/sí*
Do you speak English?	*¿habla usted inglés?*
Slower, please	*más despacio, por favor*
I am sorry, I don't speak Spanish	*Lo siento, no hablo español*
How are you?	*¿qué tal?*
I am fine	*estoy bien*
I am American (male/female)	*Soy estadounidense*
I am Australian	*Soy autraliano/a*
I am Belgian	*Soy belga*
I am British (male/female)	*Soy británico/a*
I am Canadian	*Soy canadiense*
I am German (male/female)	*Soy alemán/a*
I am Italian (male/female)	*Soy italiano/a*
I am Swiss	*Soy suizo*
I am a tourist	*Soy turista*
single (m/f)	*soltero/a*
divorced (m/f)	*divorciado/a*
married (m/f)	*casado/a*
friend (m/f)	*amigo/a*
child (m/f)	*niño/a*
husband, wife	*esposo/a*
mother, father	*madre, padre*
brother, sister	*hermano/a*
widower widow	*viudo/a*
I am hungry	*tengo hambre*
I am ill	*estoy enfermo/a*
I am thirsty	*tengo sed*

DIRECTIONS
beside	*al lado de*
to the right	*a la derecha*
to the left	*a la izquierda*
here, there	*aquí, allí*
into, inside	*dentro*

Glossary

outside	fuera
behind	detrás
in front of	delante
between	entre
far from	lejos de
Where is ... ?	¿dónde está ... ?
To get to ...?	¿para ir a...?
near	cerca de
straight ahead	todo recto

MONEY

money	dinero / plata
credit card	tarjeta de crédito
exchange	cambio
traveller's cheque	cheque de viaje
I don't have any money	no tengo dinero
The bill, please	la cuenta, por favor
receipt	recibo

SHOPPING

store	tienda
market	mercado
open, closed	abierto/a, errado/a
How much is this?	¿cuánto es?
to buy, to sell	comprar, vender
the customer	el / la cliente
salesman	vendedor
saleswoman	vendedora
I need...	necesito...
I would like...	yo quisiera...
batteries	pilas
blouse	blusa
cameras	cámaras
cosmetics and perfumes	cosméticos y perfumes
cotton	algodón
dress jacket	saco
eyeglasses	lentes, gafas
fabric	tela
film	película
gifts	regalos
gold	oro
handbag	bolsa
hat	sombrero
jewellery	joyería
leather	cuero, piel
local crafts	artesanía
magazines	revistas
newpapers	periódicos
pants	pantalones
records, cassettes	discos, casetas
sandals	sandalias
shirt	camisa

150 Glossary

shoes	zapatos
silver	plata
skirt	falda
sun screen products	productos solares
T-shirt	camiseta
watch	reloj
wool	lana

MISCELLANEOUS

a little	poco
a lot	mucho
good (m/f)	bueno/a
bad (m/f)	malo/a
beautiful (m/f)	hermoso/a
pretty (m/f)	bonito/a
ugly	feo
big	grande
tall (m/f)	alto/a
small (m/f)	pequeño/a
short (length) (m/f)	corto/a
short (person) (m/f)	bajo/a
cold (m/f)	frío/a
hot	caliente
dark (m/f)	oscuro/a
light (colour)	claro
do not touch	no tocar
expensive (m/f)	caro/a
cheap (m/f)	barato/a
fat (m/f)	gordo/a
slim, skinny (m/f)	delgado/a
heavy (m/f)	pesado/a
light (weight) (m/f)	ligero/a
less	menos
more	más
narrow (m/f)	estrecho/a
wide (m/f)	ancho/a
new (m/f)	nuevo/a
old (m/f)	viejo/a
nothing	nada
something (m/f)	algo/a
quickly	rápidamente
slowly (m/f)	despacio/a
What is this?	¿qué es esto?
when?	¿cuando?
where?	¿dónde?

TIME

in the afternoon, early evening	por la tarde
at night	por la noche
in the daytime	por el día
in the morning	por la mañana
minute	minuto
month	mes

ever	*jamás*
never	*nunca*
now	*ahora*
today	*hoy*
yesterday	*ayer*
tomorrow	*mañana*
What time is it?	*¿qué hora es?*
hour	*hora*
week	*semana*
year	*año*
Sunday	*domingo*
Monday	*lunes*
Tuesday	*martes*
Wednesday	*miércoles*
Thursday	*jueves*
Friday	*viernes*
Saturday	*sábado*
January	*enero*
February	*febrero*
March	*marzo*
April	*abril*
May	*mayo*
June	*junio*
July	*julio*
August	*agosto*
September	*septiembre*
October	*octubre*
November	*noviembre*
December	*diciembre*

WEATHER

It is cold	*hace frío*
It is warm	*hace calor*
It is very hot	*hace mucho calor*
sun	*sol*
It is sunny	*hace sol*
It is cloudy	*está nublado*
rain	*lluvia*
It is raining	*está lloviendo*
wind	*viento*
It is windy	*hay viento*
snow	*nieve*
damp	*húmedo*
dry	*seco*
storm	*tormenta*
hurricane	*huracán*

COMMUNICATION

air mail	*correos aéreo*
collect call	*llamada por cobrar*
dial the number	*marcar el número*
area code, country code	*código*

152 Glossary

envelope	*sobre*
long distance	*larga distancia*
post office	*correo*
rate	*tarifa*
stamps	*estampillas*
telegram	*telegrama*
telephone book	*un guia telefónica*
wait for the tone	*esperar la señal*

ACTIVITIES

beach	*playa*
museum or gallery	*museo*
scuba diving	*buceo*
to swim	*bañarse*
to walk around	*pasear*
hiking	*caminata*
trail	*pista, sendero*
cycling	*ciclismo*
fishing	*pesca*

TRANSPORTATION

arrival, departure	*llegada, salida*
on time	*a tiempo*
cancelled (m/f)	*anulado/a*
one way ticket	*ida*
return	*regreso*
round trip	*ida y vuelta*
schedule	*horario*
baggage	*equipajes*
north, south	*norte, sur*
east, west	*este, oeste*
avenue	*avenida*
street	*calle*
highway	*carretera*
expressway	*autopista*
airplane	*avión*
airport	*aeropuerto*
bicycle	*bicicleta*
boat	*barco*
bus	*bus*
bus stop	*parada*
bus terminal	*terminal*
train	*tren*
train crossing	*crucero ferrocarril*
station	*estación*
neighbourhood	*barrio*
collective taxi	*colectivo*
corner	*esquina*
express	*rápido*
safe	*seguro/a*
be careful	*cuidado*
car	*coche, carro*
To rent a car	*alquilar un auto*

gas	*gasolina*
gas station	*gasolinera*
no parking	*no estacionar*
no passing	*no adelantar*
parking	*parqueo*
pedestrian	*peaton*
road closed, no through traffic	*no hay paso*
slow down	*reduzca velocidad*
speed limit	*velocidad permitida*
stop	*alto*
stop! (an order)	*pare*
traffic light	*semáforo*

ACCOMMODATION

cabin, bungalow	*cabaña*
accommodation	*alojamiento*
double, for two people	*doble*
single, for one person	*sencillo*
high season	*temporada alta*
low season	*temporada baja*
bed	*cama*
floor (first, second...)	*piso*
main floor	*planta baja*
manager	*gerente, jefe*
double bed	*cama matrimonial*
cot	*camita*
bathroom	*baños*
with private bathroom	*con baño privado*
hot water	*agua caliente*
breakfast	*desayuno*
elevator	*ascensor*
air conditioning	*aire acondicionado*
fan	*ventilador, abanico*
pool	*piscina, alberca*
room	*habitación*

NUMBERS

1	uno	30	treinta
2	dos	31	treinta y uno
3	tres	32	treinta y dos
4	cuatro	40	cuarenta
5	cinco	50	cincuenta
6	seis	60	sesenta
7	siete	70	setenta
8	ocho	80	ochenta
9	nueve	90	noventa
10	diez	100	cien
11	once	101	ciento uno
12	doce	102	ciento dos
13	trece	200	doscientos
14	catorce	300	trescientos
15	quince	400	quatrocientoa
16	dieciséis	500	quinientos
17	diecisiete	600	seiscientos
18	dieciocho	700	sietecientos
19	diecinueve	800	ochocientos
20	veinte	900	novecientos
21	veintiuno	1,000	mil
22	veintidós	1,100	mil cien
23	veintitrés	1,200	mil doscientos
24	veinticuatro	2000	dos mil
25	veinticinco	3000	tres mil
26	veintiséis	10,000	diez mil
27	veintisiete	100,000	cien mil
28	veintiocho	1,000,000	un millón
29	veintinueve		

Index

Accommodations 111
Andrea
  (Playa Cofresi) 114
El Pequeño Refugio
  (Cabarete) 126
Hostal Jimesson
  (Puerto Plata) 113
Koch's Guest House
  (Sosúa) 120
La Catalina (Cabrera) . 130
Las Orquideas de
  Cabarete (Cabarete) 126
Las Palmas Beach Resort
  (Cabarete) 127
The Casa Marina Reef
  (Sosúa) 122
The Albatros
  (Cabarete) 124
The Amhsa Estrella del
  Mar (Cabarete) 127
The Apart Hotel Cita del
  Sol (Cabarete) 124
The Apart-Hotel San José
  (Río San Juan) 128
The Bahía Blanca
  (Río San Juan) 128
The Bahía Principe
  (Río San Juan) 128
The Bella Vista
  (Sosúa) 123
The Cabarete Beach Hotel
  (Cabarete) 126
The Camacho Hotel
  (Puerto Plata) 113
The Caribbean Village
  (Playa Grande) 130
The Caribe Surf Hotel
  (Cabarete) 124
The Casa Laguna
  (Cabarete) 126
The Casa Marina Beach
  Club (Sosúa) 122
The Club Marina
  (Sosúa) 122
The El Indio
  (Puerto Plata) 113
The Elizabeth
  (Playa Cofresi) 114

The Flamenco Beach
  (Playa Dorada) 115
The Garden Club
  (Playa Cofresi) 114
The Gran Ventana
  (Playa Dorada) 118
The Hacienda Resorts
  (Playa Cofresi) 114
The Heavens
  (Playa Dorada) 116
The Hotel Carib Caban
  (Nagua) 130
The Hotel Dilone
  (Puerto Plata) 113
The Jack Tar Village
  (Playa Dorada) 116
The Larimar Beach Resort
  (Sosúa) 123
The Marco Polo Club
  (Sosúa) 122
The Paradise Beach Club
  (Playa Dorada) 117
The Pension Anneliese
  (Sosúa) 120
The Pierfiorgio Palace
  Hotel (Sosúa) 121
The Playa de Oro Hotel
  (Sosúa) 123
The Playa Dorada Hotel
  (Playa Dorada) 117
The Playa Naco Resort
  (Playa Dorada) 117
The Puerto Plata
  (Puerto Plata) 113
The Puerto Plata Resort
  (Puerto Plata) 114
The Puerto Plata Village
  (Playa Dorada) 117
The Punta Goleta Beach
  Resort (Sosúa) 123
The Río San Juan Hotel
  (Río San Juan) 128
The Sol de Plata Beach
  Resort (Sosúa) 123
The Sosúa by the Sea
  (Sosúa) 121
The Sosúa Hotel
  (Sosúa) 121

156 Index

The Tropical
  (Playa Cofresi) 114
The Victoria
  (Playa Dorada) 118
The Villas de Luxe
  (Playa Cofresi) 115
The Villas Doradas
  (Playa Dorada) 118
The Voramar (Sosúa) . . 120
The Waterfront Hotel
  (Sosúa) 120
The Windsurf Resort
  (Cabarete) 124
The Yaroa (Sosúa) . . 121
Villa Taïna (Cabarete) 124
Alcázar de Colón
  (Santo Domingo) 104
Alcohol 145
Alou, Felipe 41
Amazone 2 (Cabrera) 95
Apart-hotels 112
Balneario de la Confluencia
  (Jarabacoa) 110
Balneario de la Guazaras
  (Jarabacoa) 110
Banco de la Plata Reserve
  (Puerto Plata) 89
Banking 62
Baseball 41
Beaches
  Cabarete 93
  Cabrera 76
  Costambar 89
  Costambar Beach 74
  Long Beach 74
  Nagua 76
  Playa Cabarete
    (Atlantic Coast) 75
  Playa Caletón
    (Río San Juan) 94
  Playa Carabete 75
  Playa Carleton
    (Atlantic Coast) 75
  Playa Chiquito 90
  Playa Cofresí 74
  Playa Dorada 74
  Playa Grande 76
  Playa Grande
    (Atlantic Coast) 76
  Playa Libre 75
  Playa Libre (Sosúa) . . 92
  Playa Puerto Chiquito . . 74
  Playa Punta Goleta . . . 75

Playa Sosúa 75
Playa Sosúa 91
Playa Sosúa
  (Atlantic Coast) 75
Puerto Plata 74
Punta Goleta 92
Río San Juan 75
Sosúa 75
Bed and Breakfasts 112
Birdwatching 81
Brugal Rum Distillery
  (Puerto Plata) 88
Cabañas 112
Cabarete 92
  Accommodations . . . 124
  Entertainment 144
  Restaurants 137
  Shopping 146
Cabarete beach
  (Cabarete) 93
Cabrera 95
  Accommodations . . . 130
  Restaurants 139
Calle Arzobispo Meriño
  (Santo Domingo) 106
Calle Atarazana
  (Santo Domingo) 104
Calle Isabel la Católica
  (Santo Domingo) 105
Calle Las Damas
  (Santo Domingo) 100
Cancellation Insurance 48
Capilla de Nuestra Señora
  (Santo Domingo) 103
Carnival (Santiago de Los
  Caballeros) 109
Casa de Bastidas
  (Santo Domingo) 102
Casa de Hernán Cortes
  (Santo Domingo) 102
Casa de Los Jesuitas
  (Santo Domingo) 103
Casa del Cordón
  (Santo Domingo) 105
Casa Diego Caballero
  (Santo Domingo) 100
Casa Sacramento
  (Santo Domingo) 100
Catedral Santa
  (Santo Domingo) 100
Caves (Cabarete) 93
Coach 61
Cockfighting 42

Index

Collective Taxi 61
Consulates 44
Costambar 89
Costambar Beach 74
Culture 37
Currency 62
Customs 44
Dance 39
Deep-Sea Fishing 80
Departure Tax 44
Dominican Cuisine 131
Drinks 131
Driving 56
Economy 34
El Barrio Acapulco
 (Río San Juan) 94
El Batey (Sosúa) 92
Electricity 66
Embassies 44
Entertainment 143
Entrance Formalities 43
Ermita San Anton
 (Santo Domingo) 106
Exploring 83
Fauna 14
Fax 64
Financial Services 62
Fortaleza San Felipe de
 (Puerto Plata) 84
Fortaleza Santo Domingo
 (Santo Domingo) 102
Fuerte San Diego
 (Santo Domingo) 104
Gasoline 59
Gaspar Hernández 93
Gay Life 66
Geography 12
Glorieta (Puerto Plata) 86
Golf 81
Guagua 61
Hacienda Resorts
 (Playa Cofresí) 89
Health 49
Health Insurance 48
History 17
Hitchhiking 62
Holidays 65
Horseback Riding 80
Hospital de San Nicolás
 (Santo Domingo) 107
Hostal Palacio Nicolás de
 Ovando (Santo Domingo) . 102
Hotels 111

Iglesia San Felipe
 (Puerto Plata) 86
Iglesia Santa Bárbara
 (Santo Domingo) 105
Imperial Convento
 (Santo Domingo) 107
Jarabacoa 109
 Restaurants 142
La Piscina (Río San Juan) . . 94
Lagoon (Cabarete) 93
Laguna Gri-Gri
 (Río San Juan) 94
Lifestyle 37
Literature 37
Long Beach 74
Long Beach (Puerto Plata) . 84
Los Charamicos (Sosúa) . . . 92
Mail 63
Malecón (Puerto Plata) . . . 86
Mercado Modelo
 (Santo Domingo) 108
Mercados 145
Monasterio de San Francisco
 (Santo Domingo) 106
Money 62
Motorcycle 60
Motorcyle-Taxi 60
Museo de Juan Pablo Duarte
 (Santo Domingo) 105
Museo de Las Casas Reales
 (Santo Domingo) 103
Museo de Sosúa (Sosúa) . . . 92
Museo del Ámbar
 (Puerto Plata) 86
Museo del Ámbar
 (Santo Domingo) 106
Museo del Hombre Domin-
 icano (Santo Domingo) . 108
Museum of Taino Art
 (Puerto Plata) 86
Music 39
Nagua 96
 Accommodations . . . 130
National Parks 69
 Parque Nacional
  Armando Bermudez . 71
 Parque Nacional Banco
  de la Plata 72
 Parque Nacional Cabo
  Frances Viejo 95
 Parque Nacional de
  Monte Cristi 72

158 Index

Parque Nacional
   del Este 70
Parque Nacional Isabel
   de Torres 72
Parque Nacional Isla
   Cabritos 71
Parque Nacional
   Jaragua 70
Parque Nacional José
   del Carmen Ramirez . 71
Parque Nacional La
   Caleta 70
Parque Nacional Laguna
   Rincón 71
Parque Nacional
   Los Haïtises 71
Parque Nacional Sierra
   de Bahoruco 70
Reserva Cientifica Valle
   Nuevo 71
Opening Hours 145
Outdoors 69
Ovando, Nicolas de 96
Packing 54
Painting 39
Palacio de Borgella
   (Santo Domingo) 100
Palm Tree Route 96
Panteon Nacional
   (Santo Domingo) 103
Parks
   Amazone 2 (Cabrera) . 95
   Banco de la Plata Reserve
   (Puerto Plata) 89
   Parque Central
   (Nagua) 96
   Parque Central
   (Puerto Plata) 86
   Parque Colón
   (Santo Domingo) ... 99
   Parque Duarte
   (Puerto Plata) 84
   Parque Duarte
   (Santo Domingo) .. 107
   Parque Independencia
   (Santo Domingo) .. 107
   Reserva Cientifica Isabel
   de Torres 88
Parque Central 86
Parque Central (Nagua) ... 96
Parque Colón
   (Santo Domingo) 99

Parque Duarte
   (Puerto Plata) 84
Parque Duarte
   (Santo Domingo) 107
Parque Independencia
   (Santo Domingo) 107
Parque Nacional Cabo Frances
   Viejo (Cabrera) 95
Passport 43
Petrol 59
Pico Isabel de Torres
   (Puerto Plata) 88
Playa Cabarete
   (Atlantic Coast) 75
Playa Caletón
   (Río San Juan) 94
Playa Carabete 75
Playa Cofresi
   Accommodations ... 114
Playa Cofresí 74
Playa Cofresí Beach
   (Playa Cofresí) 90
Playa Dorada 90
   Accommodations ... 115
   Entertainment 143
   Restaurants 135
   Shopping 146
Playa Dorada Beach
   (Playa Dorada) 90
Playa Grande 95
   Accommodations ... 130
Playa Grande
   (Atlantic Coast) 76
Playa Libre 75
Playa Libre (Sosúa) 92
Playa Magante 93
Playa Puerto Chiquito 74
Playa Punta Goleta 75
Playa Sosúa 75
Playa Sosúa (Atlantic Coast) 75
Playa Sosúa (Sosúa) 91
Plaza de la Cultura
   (Santo Domingo) 108
Police 59
Politics 32
Population 36
Portrait 11
Practical Information 43
Prostitution 67
Public Bus 61
Puerto Chiquito 90
Puerto Chiquito Beach
   (Playa Chiquito) 90

Puerto Plata 84
    Accommodations . . . 112
    Entertainment 143
    Restaurants 132
    Shopping 145
Puerto Plata International
Airport 47
Punta Goleta 92
Punta Goleta beach 92
Quisqueya Stadium
(Puerto Plata) 89
Rancho Baiguate
(Jarabacoa) 110
Reserva Científica Isabel de
Torres (Puerto Plata) 88
Restaurants 131
    Bahía Blanca
    (Río San Juan) 139
    Barriloche
    (Santo Domingo) . . 141
    Britania Pub (Sosúa) . 136
    Cafe de Las Flores
    (Santiago) 141
    Casa del Pescador
    (Cabarete) 138
    Casita de Papy
    (Cabarete) 138
    Don Luis
    (Jarabacoa) 142
    Helado Bon
    (Puerto Plata) 132
    Hemingway's Café
    (Playa Dorada) 135
    L'Avocat (Santiago) . . 141
    La Carreta (Sosúa) . . . 136
    La Catalina (Cabrera) 139
    La Crêpe Bretonne
    (Sosúa) 135
    La Crêperie
    (Santiago) 141
    La Ponderosa
    (Puerto Plata) 135
    La Puntilla de Pierfiorgo
    (Sosúa) 137
    Le Petit Provençal
    (Cabarete) 138
    Meson de la Cava
    (Santiago) 141
    Miró (Cabarete) 138
    PJ's (Sosúa) 136
    Plaza Cafe
    (Puerto Plata) 132
    Polanco
    (Puerto Plata) 134
    Río San Juan
    (Río San Juan) 139
    Ristorante La Briciola
    (Santo Domingo) . . 142
    Ristorante Vento
    (Cabarete) 138
    The El Toro Restaurant
    (Sosúa) 137
    The Las Brisas Restaurant
    (Cabarete) 137
    The Casona Rapida Com-
    ida (Río San Juan) . . 139
    The El Coral (Sosúa) . 136
    The Jarvis
    (Puerto Plata) 134
    The Neptune
    (Puerto Plata) 134
    The Portofino
    (Puerto Plata) 132
    The Quesos Deli
    (Río San Juan) 139
    The Rendez-Vous Café
    (Cabarete) 137
    The Romantica
    Restaurant (Sosúa) . 136
    The Waterfront
    (Sosúa) 136
Río San Juan 94
    Accommodations . . . 128
    Restaurants 139
Río San Juan Beach
(Río San Juan) 94
Safety 54
Sailing 79
Salto de Baiguate
(Jarabacoa) 110
Salto de Jimenoa
(Jarabacoa) 110
Santo Domingo 96
    Restaurants 140
Scooters 60
Security 54
Semana Santa 67
Shopping 145
    Alcohol 145
    Cabarete 146
    Mercados 145
    Opening Hours 145
    Puerto Plata 146
    Sosúa 146

Sinagoga (Sosúa) 92
Smokers 66
Snorkelling 77
Sosúa 91
    Accommodations . . . 118
    Entertainment 144
    Restaurants 135
    Shopping 146
Surfing 78
Windsurfing 78
Swimming 72
Taxes 66
Taxi 60
Telecommunications 63
Telephone 64
Tercera Ordén de los
    Dominicos 107
Theft Insurance 48
Time Change 67
Tips 66
Torre del Homenaje
    (Santo Domingo) 102
Tour Guides 65
Tourist Card 44
Tourist Offices 46
Traditions 37
Transportation 55
Universidad Santo Tomás de
    Aquino 107
Visas 44
Waterslides 80
Weights 68
Women Traveling Alone . . . 66
Youth Hostels 112
Zona Colonial
    (Santo Domingo) 99